For John Knight –

In gratitude for all you've done for me, and all the support you've given me in following my dreams –

Jennifer Leigh Selig
August 2004

D1443034

THINKING
OUTSIDE
THE
CHURCH

For my primary places of worship:
My family, home, and work

For my priests:
Jesus, Buddha, and Gandhi,
Rilke, Rumi, and Hafiz,
Martin Luther King, Jr., and Marianne Williamson

For my fellow pilgrims:
Kristen Nichols, Serra Reid, Leslie McCormick,
Shannan Brown, Mark Schaefer, Steve Steuart,
and my Pacifica peers

With special thanks to:
My beloved friend, Mike Ownbey, for providing the space
My faithful editor, Kelly Gilbert, for providing the page

THINKING OUTSIDE THE CHURCH

110 WAYS TO CONNECT WITH
YOUR SPIRITUAL NATURE

JENNIFER LEIGH SELIG, PH.D.

Andrews McMeel
Publishing
Kansas City

04 05 06 07 08   KP1   10 9 8 7 6 5 4 3 2 1

Library of Congress Cataloging-in-Publication Data

Thinking outside the church : 110 ways to connect with your spiritual
   nature / [edited by] Jennifer Leigh Selig.
      p. cm.
   ISBN 0-7407-4204-3
   1. Spiritual life. I. Selig, Jennifer Leigh.
   BL624.T455 2004
   204'4—dc22

                                                    2004047732

Book design and composition by Kelly & Company, Lee's Summit, Missouri

ATTENTION: SCHOOLS AND BUSINESSES

CONTENTS

INTRODUCTION

Who builds a church within their hearts
And takes it with them everywhere
Is holier far than they whose church
Is but a one-day house of prayer.

Morris Abel Beer

One morning when I was sitting inside a temple staring outside through the large glass doors, I noticed a sign above the door that said EXIT. In the way that my mind sometimes trips and spins of its own accord, I began to wonder about what would happen if we replaced all EXIT signs with ENTER and all ENTER signs with EXIT. How would our thinking change if we "entered" into the world through our churches and temples, if we saw ourselves as outside the world when we were inside? Would we then see the world at large as our temple, the streets and sidewalks and byways and roadways and pathways through the natural world as our real place of spiritual worship? What would our lives look like if we reversed the signs, if we exited the church to enter the church?

Thinking Outside the Church: 110 Ways to Connect with Your Spiritual Nature explores the idea inherent to a spiritual sensibility: that spirituality is everywhere and anywhere and cannot be contained or restrained inside any walls of worship. It does not deny that spirituality *can* be found when we exit the world and enter the church but only argues that this narrows our spiritual experience to four walls, a roof, and an hour of religious service on Sunday morning. To "think outside the church" means to think that everything outside the church can be found and *should* be found a spiritual experience as well. To think outside the church means to lengthen and broaden and heighten our worship in the world by expanding our definition of worship and the meaning of "religious service." Thinking outside the church is an attitude we bring to the world that seeks to see the spiritual everywhere, in all our values and activities and experiences, in all people, and in the whole of the sensual and natural worlds.

And here is the problem inherent in a book like this. Its basic premise is that the spiritual is ubiquitous and infinite, and yet it offers a finite number of spiritual pathways bound into a book. You may find yourself asking, "Why did she choose this and not that? How could she have left this out? How is this more important than that? These two things sound similar. Why did she separate them?" Please know that I asked myself these questions as well—constantly. I struggled with issues of inclusion and exclusion, of separation and definition, of prioritization and demarcation. In the end I came to see, and hope you will as well, that this book is an attempt to cultivate an attitude, not to proscribe a path, as in *Thou shalt find these things spiritual above all other things.*

In fact, I'm hoping you'll join with me and other readers of this book in making it a living, growing thing. I hope you'll visit the Web site www. thinkingoutsidethechurch.com and add your voice to mine and those authors included here. On the Web site you will be able to add your own thoughts and favorite quotes and poems to the 110 pathways in this book, but even more important, you will be able to add your own ways of connecting with spirit, thus taking what is bound and finite in this book and making it truly spiritual and truly inclusive.

And here is another problem inherent in a book like this. Its basic premise is inclusivity, and yet it uses language that excludes. Alice Walker says, "The experience of God, or in any case the possibility of experiencing God, is innate." What is *not* innate is the language we use to express our spiritual experience. For some, to call the experience of the spiritual by the name of God excludes; for others, *not* to call it God excludes. You may find yourself asking, "Why does she refer to God in a book about thinking outside the church? Why does she sometimes capitalize *Spirit* and other times not? Why does she the use the words *holy* and *divine* as if they were nouns and not adjectives? Why does she refer to religion so often in a book about spirituality?" This book is an attempt to put into feeble language the *omnipresent Unlanguagable,* which is just as good a definition of Spirit or God or the Divine or the Holy as any other. When and if it fails, cross out the words that exclude you, that make your heart cry from constriction, and write in the words that include you, that make your heart sing with expansion.

For if there is one thing this book hopes to provide, it is expansion. To think outside the church means to see all of nature as an altar, to perform any activity as worship, to hear the sensual world as a hymn, to view people as priests, to seek experience rather than dogma and make of our values a creed. I remind myself of this with a plaque nailed to the fence in my backyard that reads "The world is our cloister" (Joanna Macy). A cloister is a place of religious seclusion, often a monastery or nunnery. Thinking outside the church means that we see the world as our cloister and our lives as a holy walk into and through the wider spiritual world.

ACTIVITIES

All our acts have sacramental possibilities.

Freya Stark

Now is the time to know
That all that you do is sacred.

Hafiz

 Celebrating

Those of us with a spiritual inclination know that every day is a holy day, or at least *should* be, but let's face it, it's hard to live that way. There are our jobs, there are the daily hassles of grooming and eating, and there are all the other mundane activities that occupy us from morning to night. And yet a holy day, a *holiday,* takes us out of all of that, if only for the day. We don't go to work, the daily hassles of grooming and eating take on elevated meaning through special clothing and foods, and we set aside our mundane activities to take part in rituals that bind us to other people and older times.

Holidays are a time for celebration, and as the Quaker author Richard Foster writes, "Celebration is central to all the Spiritual Disciplines." In his book *Celebration of Discipline,* he argues that we need "joyful spirit of festivity" because "it is an occupational hazard of devout folk to become stuffy bores. This should not be. Of all people, we should be the most free, alive, interesting. Celebration adds a note of festivity and hilarity to our lives." The serious significance of spiritual holidays and celebrations was not lost on comedian Henny Youngman, who quipped, "I once wanted to become an atheist, but I gave up—they have no holidays."

Though some of the quotes below speak to specific holidays, what makes them universal is the magic known as *the holiday spirit,* a spirit that transcends the name, date, culture, or cause of celebration.

The highest human purpose is always
to reinvent and celebrate the sacred.

N. Scott Momaday

Christmas is not a time nor a season, but a state of mind.
To cherish peace and goodwill, to be plenteous in mercy,
is to have the real spirit of Christmas.

Calvin Coolidge

Blessed is the season which engages the
whole world in a conspiracy of love.

Hamilton Wright Mabie

The spirit of the powwow is a continuum in Indian life. It isn't just
for a few days in March. We live this spirit on a daily basis. It is why we
have survived for so long. At one time we were a forgotten people, but
I think we are getting stronger. From the powwow we gain strength as
Indian people, individually and collectively, to go on into the twenty-
first century.

Taos Pueblo Indian Linday Yardley

To many people holidays are not voyages of discovery,
but a ritual of reassurance.

Philip Andrew Adams

The more you praise and celebrate your life,
the more there is in life to celebrate.

Oprah Winfrey

Celebrate the happiness that friends are always giving.
Make every day a holiday and celebrate just living!

Amanda Bradley

Life is meant to be a celebration! It shouldn't be necessary
to set aside special times to remind us of this fact. Wise is the
person who finds a reason to make every day a special one.

Leo Buscaglia

Celebrations are the juice of life.

John D. Hofbrauer, Jr.

Take hold of your own life.
See that the whole existence is celebrating.
These trees are not serious, these birds are not serious.
The rivers and the oceans are wild,
and everywhere there is fun,
everywhere there is joy and delight.
Watch existence,
listen to the existence and become part of it.

Osho

Cooking and Dining

The Jewish holy book the Talmud says: "Hospitality is one form of worship."
When we cook for others, when we prepare a meal for them, we minister
to their bodies, to their senses, and to their spirits. We take our precious
time and energy—manifestations of our spirits—and we fashion out of
nature's resources of food and wine an altar, a holy table, where we take
our daily bread together in sacred communion. Nothing is so basic and
necessary as eating and drinking, making them a perfect pathway of worship and devotion, everyday rituals that we can infuse with spirituality.

COOKING

A cook, when I dine, seems to me a divine being, who from the depths
of his kitchen rules the human race. One considers him as a minister of
heaven, because his kitchen is a temple, in which his ovens are the altar.

Marc-Antoine Désaugiers

The preparation of food also serves the soul in a number of ways. In a general sense, it gives us a valuable, ordinary opportunity to meditate quietly, as we peel and cut vegetables, stir pots, measure out proportions, and watch for boiling and roasting. We can become absorbed in the sensual contemplation of colors, textures, and tastes as, alchemists of the kitchen, we mix and stir just the right proportions. The colors and smells can take us out of "real" time, which can be so deadening, and lift us into another time and space altogether, the time of myth created by cooking. The kitchen is one of the most soulful rooms in a house.

Thomas Moore

Our lives are not in the lap of the gods, but in the lap of our cooks.

Lin Yutang

We may live without poetry, music, and art; We may live without conscience, and live without heart; We may live without friends; we may live without books; But civilized man cannot live without cooks.

Owen Meredith

The preparation of good food is merely another expression of art, one of the joys of civilized living.

Dione Lucas

Cooking is like love.
It should be entered into with abandon or not at all.

Harriet Van Horne

For those who love it, cooking is at once child's play and adult joy. And cooking done with care is an act of love.

Craig Claiborne

The home is a sacred place where you can communicate with the four elements of the universe: earth, water, air, and fire. You mix it with your love and emotions to create magic. Through cooking, you raise your spiritual level and balance yourself in a world that is materialistic.

Laura Esquivel

My kitchen is a mystical place, a kind of temple for me. It is a place where the surfaces seem to have significance, where the sounds and odors carry meaning that transfers from the past and bridges to the future.

Pearl Bailey

DINING

A meal, however simple, is a moment of intersection. It is at once the most basic, the most fundamental, of our life's activities, maintaining the life of our bodies; shared with others it can be an occasion of joy and communion, uniting people deeply.

Elise Boulding

I learned early on that setting a table is so much more than just laying down knives and forks. It is creating a setting for food and conversation, setting a mood and an aura that lingers long after what was served and who said what was forgotten.

Peri Wolfman

Sharing food with another human being is an intimate act that should not be indulged in lightly.

M. F. K. Fisher

Dining is and always was a great artistic opportunity.

Frank Lloyd Wright

There is one practice which any family can maintain and that is the practice of a time of worship at each family meal. Nearly all families are together for at least one meal a day and, in any case, should sacrifice much else to make this possible. The table is really the family altar! Here those of all ages come together and help to sustain both their physical and their spiritual existence. If a sacrament is "an actual conveyance of spiritual meaning and power by a material process," then a family meal can be a sacrament. It entwines the material and the spiritual in a remarkable way.

Elton Trueblood

A lot of us eat most of our meals alone at a desk or standing up at a counter somewhere. And I think at some level we realize this is a kind of soulless way to feed ourselves. Eating together, a communal meal, is a soul moment.

Phil Cousineau

Later in the day, as we sit down to dinner, my wife and I hold hands before we eat. As we look in each other's eyes, we tell each other without words that we love each other very much. That moment of stopping and holding hands is a powerful statement of affection and well-being. If we have company, we tell them that the finest blessing of any meal is to share it with friends, and invite them to join us in our ritual.

Robert Fulghum

One cannot think well, love well, sleep well, if one has not dined well.

Virginia Woolf

Eating a meal with full awareness can be a powerful, enlightening, and healing experience.

David Simon

Enchant, stay beautiful and graceful, but do this, eat well. Bring the same consideration to the preparation of your food as you devote to your appearance. Let your dinner be a poem, like your dress.

Charles Pierre Monselet

Eating is not merely a material pleasure. Eating well gives a spectacular joy to life and contributes immensely to goodwill and happy companionship. It is of great importance to the morale.

Elsa Schiaparelli

When we develop reverence for food and the miracle of transformation inherent in it, just the simple act of eating creates a ritual of celebration.

Deepak Chopra

 **Daily Living**

There is a Zen story of a monk who once asked his Master, "No matter what lies ahead, what is the Way?" The Master quickly replied, "The Way is your daily life." This idea is at the very center of the Way of Zen, which also gave us the maxim "Before enlightenment, chop wood, carry water. After enlightenment, chop wood, carry water." The spiritual path is not an extraordinary path, not a path that leads us *out* of our everyday existence, but is instead quite an ordinary path that leads us *into* our existence with eyes capable of seeing everything as holy, of seeing everything as an opportunity for union with the divine. Our outer tasks won't change—we'll still chop wood and carry water—but we will do so with an enlightened consciousness.

Popular spiritual writer Thomas Moore points out that this is not just a Zen way of thinking but is a common belief in many religions and spiritual systems. "While many people seem bent on achieving extraordinary levels of consciousness and great powers of spirit, religions also teach the holiness of the commonplace. It isn't easy in our complicated world to enjoy the pleasures of ordinary living—children, family, neighborhood, nature, walking, gathering, eating together. I imagine life not as an ambitious quest, but as an anti-quest, a search for the ordinary and a cultivation of the unexceptional."

That anti-quest may be the hardest quest of our lives, yet it is the most important quest for those of us truly seeking to be connected with our spiritual natures.

You are to gather up the joys and sorrows, the struggles, the beauty, love, dreams and hopes of every hour that they may be consecrated at the altar of daily life.

Macrina Wiederkehr

To be really great in little things, to be truly noble and heroic in the insipid details of everyday life, is a virtue so rare as to be worthy of canonization.

Harriet Beecher Stowe

If you love the sacred and despise the ordinary, you are still bobbing in the ocean of delusion.

Lin-chi

The very commonplaces of life are components of its eternal mystery.

Gertrude Atherton

It is while you are patiently toiling at the little tasks of life that the meaning and shape of the great whole of life dawns on you.

Phillips Brooks

A monk said to Joshu, "I have just entered this monastery.
Please teach me."
"Have you eaten your rice porridge?" asked Joshu.
"Yes, I have," replied the monk.
"Then you had better wash your bowl," said Joshu.
With this the monk gained enlightenment.

Zen parable

One should hallow all that one does in one's natural life. One eats in holiness, tastes the taste of food in holiness, and the table becomes an altar. One works in holiness, and raises up the sparks which hide themselves in all tools. One walks in holiness across the fields, and the soft songs of all herbs, which they voice to God, enter into the song of our soul.

Martin Buber

If we are rooted in the belief that everything God created is potentially holy, we have the capacity to notice that which is beautiful and holy in everyday life. Everything can be seen as a miracle, part of God's plan. And when we can truly see this, we nourish our souls.

Rabbi Harold Kushner

Inward spiritual practices such as meditation, breathing techniques, and self-analysis generate insights and enhance abilities, but none are so useful as learning to live harmoniously in a committed relationship, being a skillful parent, or juggling the demands of daily life.

Dan Millman

There is no enlightenment outside of daily life.

Thich Nhat Hanh

Your daily life is your temple and your religion.
Whenever you enter into it take with you your all.

Kahlil Gibran

If your everyday life seems poor, don't
blame it; blame yourself; admit to
yourself that you are not enough of a poet
to call forth its riches; because for the
creator there is no poverty and no poor
indifferent place.

Rainer Maria Rilke

O Lord God, we pray that we may be inspired to nobleness of life in
the least things. May we dignify all our daily life. May we set such a
sacredness upon every part of our life, that nothing shall be trivial,
nothing unimportant, and nothing dull, in the daily round.

Henry Ward Beecher

Dancing

My friend Leslie McCormick is a poet, dancer, and Buddhist and is one of
the most gentle souls I know. To see her dance is to experience the illimitable beauty of her spirit, and more, to know the inexhaustible beauty of
the human spirit as it pours forth like light from the body. She once
described to me how dancing connected her to spirit. "For me, dancing
is a way of connecting with the pure, raw life force that is common to all

living things. When I am truly dancing, the mind that would otherwise wonder, 'Does this look silly?' or 'Is this beautiful enough?' is absorbed and dissolved by the mind that simply exists, the mind that connects intricately with the impulses of the body and spirit. It's an experience of myself that is free of concepts—especially expectations, assumptions, fear, and pretense. I am temporarily free of impressions of myself, of this and not that, of what is me and what is not me. To experience myself in this expanded way is, ironically, deeply self-affirming."

What Leslie describes is echoed by choreographer and dancer Judith Jamison in her book *Dancing Spirit*. "Dance is bigger than the physical body. . . . When you extend your arm, it doesn't stop at the end of your fingers, because you're dancing bigger than that; you're dancing spirit." Dancing allows us to leave ego behind, to move with freedom, to express emotions, to sway with spirit, and to make "poetry with arms and legs" (Charles Baudelaire).

We look at the dance to impart the sensation of living in an affirmation of life, to energize the spectator into keener awareness of the vigor, the mystery, the humor, the variety, and the wonder of life.

Martha Graham

The dance is the only form of magic which has not lost its ancient power. Much of it has been drawn off into religion or psychology, but nothing has yet usurped the place of the magic experience which one receives today when one lets go of oneself in rhythmic bodily movement to enter into ecstasy; and this can still be experienced, even in these times, if one treats the art as a genuinely holy activity and not as a cheap and tawdry form of entertainment.

Ted Shawn

I would believe only in a God that knows how to Dance.

Friedrich Nietzsche

Dancing is the loftiest, the most moving, the most beautiful of the arts, because it is no mere translation or abstraction from life; it is life itself.

Havelock Ellis

I experience and nurture my soul when I'm dancing, because for me, dancing is both the flight of my body and the incarnation of my spirit. It is a union of spirit and body. My soul is the bridge.

Marion Woodman

Dance is an art that imprints on the soul. It is with you every moment, it expresses itself in every thing you do.

Shirley Maclaine

Dancers are the athletes of God.

Albert Einstein

To watch us dance is to hear our hearts speak.

Hopi saying

The earth braces itself for the feet
Of a lover of God about to Dance.

Hafiz

 # Doing

Martin Luther King, Jr., talked about something he called "divine dissatisfaction." He called upon the citizens of the United States to stay in a state of divine dissatisfaction "until America will no longer have a high blood pressure of creeds and an anemia of deeds." He died in love with the creeds of his country but dissatisfied with its deeds.

I love his use of the phrase *divine dissatisfaction* in this context. I love what he is implying, that the divine is present when our beliefs match our behaviors, when our words match our actions, when we are able to walk our talk. In fact, it may be that speaking and acting are not on equal footing, for as the cliché goes, "actions speak louder than words." Thomas Jefferson, whom King greatly admired for his creeds, said something similar when he stated "It is in our lives and not our words that our religion must be read."

Saint Francis of Assisi made words an even less important part of the equation when he admonished us to "Preach the gospel all the time. If necessary use words." Preaching is not about professing, Saint Francis is saying, but about doing what one professes; then the doing itself becomes a profession. People who wish to be connected to their spirituality will examine what they do and what it professes to the world about what they believe, and they will find themselves in a state of satisfaction when the two are in sync.

> However many holy words you read, however many you speak,
> what good will they do if you do not act upon them?
>
> the Dhammapada

> The world is imprisoned in its own activity, except when actions are
> performed as worship of God. Therefore you must perform every
> action sacramentally . . . and be free from all attachment to results.
>
> the Bhagavad Gita

Faith is not only daring to believe, it is also daring to act. When I believe in myself as a son of God, I attribute to all people the same quality. This goes for people of every class, creed, and color. The proof that I believe this way will be measured by the way I act towards others. . . . To me God is all the goodness in the universe, available to me here and now, and it is up to me to help convert that goodness into action.

Wilferd A. Peterson

In the Native way we are encouraged to recognize that every moment is a sacred moment, and every action, when imbued with dedication and commitment to benefit all beings, is a sacred act.

Dhyani Ywahoo

If we do all our acts, small and great, every moment, for the sake of the whole human race, as representing the Supreme Self, then every cell and fibre of the body and inner man will be turned in one direction, resulting in perfect concentration.

William Q. Judge

I should not despise the small act. Every small act, if you do it deeply, can touch the whole universe. My small act, your small act, millions of small acts will build a wonderful world. You can move the hearts of thousands of people.

Sister Chân Không

People's dreams are made out of what they do all day. The same way a dog that runs after rabbits will dream of rabbits. It's what you do that makes your soul, not the other way around.

Barbara Kingsolver

Good actions are the invisible hinges on the doors of heaven.

Victor Hugo

Young people say, What is the sense of our small effort? They cannot see that they must lay one brick at a time; we can be responsible only for the one action at the present moment. But we can beg for an increase of love in our hearts that will vitalize and transform all our individual actions, and know that God will take them and multiply them, as Jesus multiplied the loaves and fishes.

Dorothy Day

No one can write their real religious life with pen or pencil. It is written only in actions, and its seal is our character, not our orthodoxy. Whether we, our neighbor, or God is the judge, absolutely the only value of our religious life to ourselves or to anyone is what it fits us for and enables us to do.

Wilfred T. Grenfell

 Flying

I knew I was going to love Sue Monk Kidd's novel *The Secret Life of Bees*, when in the very first paragraph, the main character lies in bed at night watching in wonder as bees squeeze through the cracks of her bedroom wall and fly around the room. No, I did not love this because I have a bee fetish, because frankly, I find the image creepy at best, terrifying at worst. But it was the way she described the flight: "I watched their wings shining like bits of chrome in the dark and felt the longing build in my chest. The way those bees flew, not even looking for a flower, just flying for the feel of the wind, split my heart down its seam."

For those of us whose hearts resonate with flying, that feeling is one we easily recognize. The longing for flight, for flying just for the feel of the wind and for the view from above, can split our hearts open and make our spirits soar. We may find our spirits take wing when we ourselves fly, whether on a plane or a hot air balloon or with a sail or parachute behind us, or we may find it when we contemplate the flight of the birds—or even the bees!

What happiness this is: to fly, skimming over the earth just as we do in our dreams! Life has become a dream. Can this be the meaning of paradise?

Nikos Kazantzakis

Can the magic of flight ever be carried by words? I think not.

Michael Parfit

The air up there in the clouds is very pure and fine, bracing and delicious. And why shouldn't it be?—it is the same the angels breathe.

Mark Twain

The natural function of the wing is to soar upwards and carry that which is heavy up to the place where dwells the race of gods. More than any other thing that pertains to the body it partakes of the nature of the divine.

Plato

It's wonderful to climb the liquid mountains of the sky. Behind me and before me is God and I have no fears.

Helen Keller

Even before [we] . . . had reached 300 feet, I recognized that the sky would be my home. I tumbled out of the airplane with stars in my eyes.

Geraldyn Cobb

Until now I have never really lived! Life on earth is a creeping, crawling business. It is in the air that one feels the glory of being a man and of conquering the elements. There is an exquisite smoothness of motion and the joy of gliding through space. It is wonderful!

Gabriele D'Annunzio

Flying is a lot like playing a musical instrument; you're doing so many things and thinking of so many other things, all at the same time. It becomes a spiritual experience. Something wonderful happens in the pit of your stomach.

Dusty McTavish

Flight is romance—not in the sense of sexual attraction, but as an experience that enriches life.

Stephen Coonts

In our dreams we are able to fly . . . and that is a remembering of how we were meant to be.

Madeleine L'Engle

In order to invent the airplane you must have at least a thousand years' experience dreaming of angels.

Arnold Rockman

 Gardening

There is no better way than gardening to be in touch and in tune with the ever-changing nature of Nature, and in turn, to have a hand in that change; as Bob Rodale points out, "To be the agent whose touch changes nature from a wild force to a work of art is inspiration of the highest order." Although plucking out weeds, although digging in dirt, although trimming and tending and pruning and planting and mowing and mulching may not seem like high art to some people, those who love gardening will tell you it isn't so, that they sweat and toil with seed and soil knowing that "to cultivate a garden is to walk with God" (Christian Nestell Bovee). Those who love gardening agree, regardless of any religious affiliation, that God was right in choosing a garden as the setting of Eden.

In the garden the door is always open into the "holy"—growth, birth, death. Every flower holds the whole mystery in its short cycle, and in the garden we are never far away from death, the fertilizing, good, creative death.

May Sarton

I prefer to their dogma my excursions into the natural gardens where the voice of the Great Spirit is heard in the twittering of birds, the rippling of mighty waters, and the sweet breathing of flowers. If this is Paganism, then at present, at least, I am a Pagan.

Zitkala-Sa

There is a kind of immortality in every garden.

Gladys Taber

I think that gardening is nearer to godliness than theology.

Vigen Guroian

In the Quran it says that believers will be rewarded with the splendors and bountiful beauty of paradise, which is described as gardens in heaven. Believers are promised gardens of heaven that have gushing fountains and flowing springs, fruit trees, and couches to recline in under the cool shade of trees.

The Muslim News

One is nearer God's heart in a garden
Than anywhere else on earth.

Dorothy Frances Gurney

Almost any garden, if you see it at just the right moment,
can be confused with paradise.

Henry Mitchell

Connection with gardens, even small ones, even potted plants, can become windows to the inner life. The simple act of stopping and looking at the beauty around us can be prayer.

Patricia R. Barrett

The best place to seek God is in a garden. You can dig for him there.

George Bernard Shaw

Gardening is not a rational act. What matters is the immersion of the hands in the earth, that ancient ceremony of which the Pope kissing the tarmac is merely a pallid vestigial remnant.

Margaret Atwood

I knew in my heart that I wanted to know the garden intimately, to
know all the flowers in each season, to be there from spring through
autumn, digging, pruning, planting, feeding, rejoicing. In short,
I had fallen in love.

Elizabeth Murray

Everything that slows us down and forces patience, everything that
sets us back into the slow cycle of nature, is a help. Gardening is
an instrument of grace.

May Sarton

 Giving

There is a story by an unknown author that I've seen circulating on the
Internet called "The Wise Woman's Stone." In it, a wise woman who was
traveling in the mountains found a precious stone in a stream. The next
day she met another traveler who was hungry, and the wise woman
opened her bag to share her food. The hungry traveler saw the precious
stone and asked the woman to give it to him. She did so without hesita-
tion. The traveler left, rejoicing in his good fortune. He knew the stone
was worth enough to give him security for a lifetime. But a few days later
he came back to return the stone to the wise woman.

"I've been thinking," he said. "I know how valuable the stone is, but I
give it back in the hope that you can give me something even more precious.
Give me what you have within you that enabled you to give me the stone."

I love this story, love the idea that while *what* we give is precious, *that*
we give is even more precious. The Bible teaches "freely you have received,
so freely give." In freely giving we acknowledge the magnanimous nature
of the spiritual world and become a conduit to unleash and release that
spirit, becoming wiser as we in turn engender the wisdom of others.

In this world always take the position of the giver. Give everything and look for no returns. Give love, give help, give service, give any little thing you can, but *keep out barter*. Make no conditions and none will be imposed. Let us give out of our own bounty, just as God gives to us. The Lord is the only Giver, all the world are only shopkeepers. Get His cheque and it must be honoured everywhere.

Swami Vivekananda

Spiritual love is a position of standing with one hand extended into the universe and one hand extended into the world, letting ourselves be a conduit for passing energy.

Christina Baldwin

We all should give what we have decided in our hearts to give, not reluctantly or under compulsion, for God loves a cheerful giver.

2 Corinthians 9:7

There are those who give little of the much they have—and they give it for recognition and their hidden desire makes their gifts unwholesome.
And there are those who have little and give it all.
There are those believers in life and the bounty of life,
and their coffer is never empty.
There are those who give with joy, and that joy is their reward.
And there are those who give with pain, and that pain is their baptism.
And there are those who give and know not pain in giving, nor do they seek joy, nor give with mindfulness of virtue;
They give as in yonder valley the myrtle breathes its fragrance into space.
Through the hands of such as these God speaks, and from behind their eyes He smiles upon the earth.

Kahlil Gibran

The more we have given to ourselves, the more we have to give to others. When we find that place within ourselves that is giving, we begin to create an outward flow. Giving to others comes not from a sense of sacrifice, self-righteousness, or spirituality, but for the pure pleasure of it, because it's fun. Giving can only come from a full, loving space.

Shakti Gawain

Not he who has much is rich, but he who gives much.

Erich Fromm

Open your eyes and look for a human being, or some work devoted to human welfare, which needs from someone a little time or friendliness, a little sympathy, or sociability, or labor. There may be a solitary or an embittered fellowman, an invalid, or an inefficient person to whom you can be something. Perhaps it is an old person or a child. Or some good work needs volunteers who can offer a free evening, or run errands. Who can enumerate the many ways in which that costly piece of working capital, a human being, can be employed? More of him is wanted everywhere! Search, then, for some investment for your humanity, and do not be frightened away if you have to wait, or to be taken on trial. And be prepared for disappointments. But in any case, do not be without some secondary work in which you can give yourself as a man to men.

It is marked out for you, if you only truly will to have it.

Albert Schweitzer

 **Healing**

The connection between healing and the divine is ancient. In many cultures, mortals learn their healing skills directly from the gods—think of Aesclepious, the first Greek healer who was the son of the god Apollo. In many cultures, healers derive their powers from their contact with the spirit world—think of curanderas and shamans. In many cultures, the divine *is* a healer—think of the healing miracles Jesus performed. Even in our medicalized Western culture, doctors are often revered as the nearest thing to gods. The ancient Roman orator Cicero is right: "In nothing do men approach so nearly to the gods, as in giving health to men." Or, I might add, in giving healing to ourselves, for we are learning that true healing comes as much from the power of our spirits within as it does from any outside power. Whether we work with our spirits to heal ourselves, or work with the divine spirit to heal others, we tap into an ancient source of spiritual connection and power when we engage in healing.

A true healer is someone through whom the innermost self, God, or Mystery can appear to you in a form in which you can receive it. Every person who comes to a true healer finds a way for his or her faith to grow in the healing presence of that person.

Richard Moss

Healing is impossible in loneliness; it is the opposite of loneliness. Conviviality is healing. To be healed we must come with all the other creatures to the feast of Creation.

Wendell Berry

The Lord does the healing. I don't heal. That's why I say prayer. I ask the Lord to intervene. It's said that Hawaiian massage is praying work.

Margaret Machado

To pity distress is but human; to relieve it is Godlike.

Horace Mann

Seek healing, a refilling of energy and spirit, as soon as you see that you need it. You don't have to push yourself to give, do, or perform when what your body, mind, soul, and emotions need is to heal.

Melody Beattie

Because our thoughts and emotions play a role in the development of an illness and because positive thoughts can increase our capacity to heal, the healing arts have turned from an exclusive focus on external medicines to a concern with one's internal, mental, and spiritual nature.

Carolyn Myss

Those who know how to go in search of the fragmented soul are healers. . . . The healer becomes a guide, someone who knows that injury to the soul means the soul has taken flight. The healer teaches you to fly to recover your soul.

Rudolfo Anaya

There is a light in this world, a healing spirit more powerful than any darkness we may encounter. We sometimes lose sight of this force when there is suffering, and too much pain. Then suddenly, the spirit will emerge through the lives of ordinary people who hear a call and answer in extraordinary ways.

Mother Teresa

The healing of our present woundedness may lie in recognizing and reclaiming the capacity we all have to heal each other, the enormous power in the simplest of human relationships: the strength of a touch, the blessing of forgiveness, the grace of someone else taking you just as you are and finding in you an unsuspected goodness.

Rachel Naomi Remen

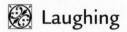 Laughing

Author and humorist Richard Lederer writes, "An Apache myth tells us that the Creator made man able to walk and talk, to see and hear—to do everything. But the Creator wasn't satisfied. Finally he made man laugh, and when man laughed and laughed, the Creator said, 'Now you are fit to live.' In Navajo culture, there is something called the First Laugh Ceremony. Tradition dictates that each Navajo baby is kept on a cradle board until he or she laughs for the first time. Then the tribe throws a celebration in honor of the child's first laugh, which is considered to be his or her birth as a social being. We are not only Homo sapiens, the creature who thinks. We are Homo guffawus, the creature who laughs."

I had the pleasure of spending time in the presence of the Dalai Lama, and what I remember the most about him, perhaps because it was the most surprising and unexpected, was his quick and constant laughter, most often at his own expense. I am not alone in my observation of him—most everyone who has spent any time around His Holiness will comment about his sense of humor; if it is true, as Pierre Delattre states, that levity and not gravity is the Tibetan way to enlightenment, then it is easy to see why the Dalai Lama is so enlightened! Crossing spiritual traditions, he took the advice of Krishna, who said, "Be a God and laugh at yourself."

A Jester may be first in the Kingdom of Heaven, because he has diminished the sadness of human life.

Rabbi Max Nussbaum

Humor is wonderful food for the soul. Too much seriousness violates the laws of nature. Living a humorless life, turning a blind eye to the paradoxes around and within us, or never even laughing at ourselves shrinks the soul.

Matthew Fox

I believe in a God who has an impish sense of humor.

Martin B. Copenhauer

Laughter can be more satisfying than honor; more precious than money; more heart-cleansing than prayer.

Harriet Rochlin

He deserves Paradise who makes his companions laugh.

the Koran

The gods too are fond of a joke.

Aristotle

When I started doing my humor ministry a reporter asked me why I was doing this. I told him the truth. God wants us to lighten up. He wants us to be joyful, cheerful, and happy. He's loving and merciful and He wants what's best for us—joy, cheerfulness, and happiness are best. God loves us. He wants our lives free of stress, tension, and anxiety. So I guess I'm a monk with a mission. . . . I pray that people will lighten up, that they'll laugh more, that they'll give humor a more important place in their lives. These are my prayers. Of course, I pray cheerfully and laugh a little while I'm praying!

Brother Craig

Humor has the same effect on your psyche and spirit as physical exercise has on our muscles.

Dr. Donald Ardell

Humor is the prelude to faith, and laughter is the beginning of prayer.

Reinhold Neibuhr

Laughter, indeed, is God's therapy.

Malcolm Muggeridge

When you laugh, you get a glimpse of God.

Merrily Belgum

God always has another custard pie up his sleeve.

Lynn Redgrave

Time spent laughing is time spent with the Gods.

Japanese proverb

 Learning and Education

I am tickled by the phrase *formal education*. I can't think of a more un-
pleasant expression for the joy of learning, one that is more stifling to the
spirit. Having been a teacher for fifteen years, I can assure you that what
happens in the classroom is anything but formal! I prefer Robert J. Sar-
dello's description of education: "Who can deny experiencing an impulse
for learning, a force welling up from within, a powerful, autonomous urge,
satisfied only through release, and when released producing an intense
form of pleasure that can only be called joy? . . . The impulse for learning
originates in an alluring display of things of the world, evoking desire for
union with them—an urge toward intimacy with the spirit, soul, vitality,

the particular beauty marking each thing as standing forth from an abyss of holiness."

What if we replaced the concept of twelve mandatory years of formal education with twelve years of exploring the abyss of holiness? What if we learned with a different goal in mind: not to regurgitate correct answers on formal standardized tests, but to experience joy, union, and intimacy with the things of the world?

Would anyone ever drop out? Wouldn't everyone want to drop in?

Learning is superior to beauty; learning is better than hidden treasure; learning is a companion on a journey to a strange country; learning is strength inexhaustible.

Hitopadesa

The ink of the scholar is more sacred than the blood of the martyr.

Mohammed

When I learn something new—and it happens every day—I feel a little more at home in this universe, a little more comfortable in the nest.

Bill Moyers

From the moment of birth, life is a process of learning. It is the chief obligation of all living things, their chief task and chief joy. . . . All things rejoice in learning, dolphins and dogs bodily smiling at the task. . . . For whatever reason we learn—from desire, from compulsions, from pride, from greed, for use, for pay—we gain joy.

Donald Cowan

Develop a passion for learning. If you do, you'll never cease to grow.

Anthony J. D'Angelo

Learning is a natural pleasure, inborn and instinctive, one of the earliest pleasures and one of the essential pleasures of the human race.

Gilbert Highet

The one activity of which the human person is capable that does not dim with age nor fail with sickness, persecution, or disgrace is learning. To learn does not mean one has to be brilliant or original, well informed or keenly rational. To learn is to take an aspect of the world into one's mind, to regard it with interest and delight, finding in contemplation its true significance, and allowing it to lead one to a new territory.

Louise Cowan

Every education is a kind of inward journey.

Vaclav Havel

Education is the movement from darkness to light.

Allan Bloom

What sculpture is to a block of marble, education is to an human soul.

Joseph Addison

You don't need me to tell you what education is. Everybody really knows that education goes on all the time everywhere all through our lives, and that it is the process of waking up to life. . . . It's not that we want to sleep our lives away. It's that it requires certain kinds of energy, certain capacities for taking the world into our consciousness, certain real powers of body and soul to be a match for reality. That's why knowledge and consciousness are two quite different things.

Mary Caroline Richards

Education is simply the soul of a society as it passes
from one generation to another.

G. K. Chesterton

The true purpose of education is to cherish and unfold the seed of
immortality already sown within us; to develop, to their fullest extent,
the capacities of every kind with which the God who made us has
endowed us.

Anna Jameson

 ## Making Love

Perhaps with tongue in cheek (or perhaps not!), Don Schrader notes, "To
hear many religious people talk, one would think God created the torso,
head, legs, and arms but the devil slapped on the genitals." In contrast,
there are many religions and spiritualities that believe exactly the opposite, that lovemaking is sacred, a blessing bestowed by God or the gods to
humanity. In *The Mythology of Sex,* Sarah Denning explains that for Eastern
cultures, "sex has not only been regarded as natural and beneficial to
health, but, for centuries, it has been used as a way of expanding and exploring spirituality." In China, she tells us, sex is referred to as "provoking
the spirit"; in India, "Hindu divinities come in pairs, often eternally con-
joined in blissful sexual embrace"; in Tantric traditions, a human can
become divine through making love by tapping into sacred sources of
creative and sexual energy, thus transforming into a god or goddess while
making love to another. Perhaps this is why we whisper and moan and
sometimes shout "Oh God! Oh my God!" at supreme moments of pleasure!

I kiss my husband and go directly to God.

Marilyn Atteberry

Making love to each other,
we worshipped the miracle of what was possible.

Alice Walker

When sex is of the Holy Spirit, it is a deepening of communication.
When it is of the ego, it is a substitute for communication. The Holy
Spirit uses sex to heal us; the ego uses it to wound us. . . . It is only
when sex is a vehicle for spiritual communion that it is truly loving,
that it joins us to another person. Then it is a sacred act.

Marianne Williamson

We should rise up and praise when we talk about what friendship is
and love is and what lovers are about—this interpenetration of one
another's souls by way of the body. That's so marvelous! I think angels
are envious of humans because we have bodies; they don't, and
lovemaking makes the angels flap their wings in envy. . . . Human
sexuality is a mystical moment in the history of the Universe. All the
angels and all the other beings come out to wonder at this.

Matthew Fox

All lovemaking (as distinct from "having sex") is Christ meeting Christ.
Love beds are altars. People are temples encountering temples, the holy
of holies receiving the holy of holies.

Andrew Harvey

Making love? It's a communion with a woman. The bed is the holy
table. There I find passion—and purification.

Omar Sharif

Is there anything else two beings can do, joined for the moment and forever in the communion of love, besides feel the depths of that mystery and remain silent? This is the point, the marvelous limit, where the Word breaks off, defeated, and the pure act triumphs. Beyond this threshold, no word sounds.

Pierre Mabille

Sex brings living beings into the world, but it also invites the vitality and exuberance of sheer life. Sex is infinitely more than the biological, because it is one of the most potent and creative manifestations of the soul. Sex has an abundance of soul.

Thomas Moore

The sexual embrace, worthily understood, can only be compared with music and with prayer.

James Hilton

The path to spiritual awakening lies within the ecstasy of true sexual fulfillment.

Sarah Denning

Sex is the religion of a marriage. It is its contemplation, its ritual, its prayer, and its communion.

Thomas Moore

Sex lies at the root of life, and we can never learn reverence for life until we learn reverence for sex.

Havelock Ellis

 Meditating

In the summer of 2003, *Time* magazine did a big cover story on meditation. According to their statistics, over 10 million Americans are meditating now. Scientific studies on the benefits of meditation are plentiful, showing that it can boost the immune system, rewire the brain to reduce stress, reduce chronic pain, and even restore psychic balance in disturbances like depression and ADD. Because of the growing body of proof regarding the multitude of benefits, meditation is being offered in schools, hospitals, law firms, government buildings, corporate offices, and prisons. Books, magazines, workshops, classes, and meditation spaces can be found everywhere.

What I found most interesting about the article was how quick it was to point out how secular meditation has become: It has detached from Zen and Buddhism and has gone mainstream, and practitioners of any faith, or *no* faith, are taking it up en masse. That's a good thing, simply because meditation, regardless of one's spirituality, is a good thing (and we've got the studies to prove it!). But let's not throw out the baby with the bathwater, so to speak. Meditators for millennia have known that it is good for the body (no scientific studies needed!), but what is more important, they have known that it is good for the spirit inside the body. Ancient wisdom is often good science, and always, what's truly good for the body is truly good for the spirit.

Meditation is in truth higher than thought. The earth seems to rest in silent meditation; and the waters and the mountains and the sky and the heavens seem all to be in meditation. Whenever a man attains greatness on this earth he has his reward according to his meditation.

the Upanishads

Praying is talking to God but meditating is listening to God.

Jeanne Adleman

There are several things we can do to stay in touch with our soul. The most important thing is to go within. This doesn't have to be formal Eastern meditation. You can meditate with your eyes open. You can meditate while walking or being close to nature. The purpose is to remind yourself of your true nature, which is that of a spiritual being. You are not your body. Your body is like a car, and you're the driver. As you find your true nature, you find that you are really being of love. And when you think about it, you see that everyone else is, too.

Brian Weiss

First, we would do well to emphasize once again the need for meditation in the life of anyone who seeks to make progress in the journey to God. This need is for a meditation that is a prayerful reflection upon the Word of God and also for meditation that, in the centering tradition, brings one into the presence of God within.

Keith Egan

The purpose of meditation is to awaken in us the sky-like nature of mind, and to introduce us to that which we really are, our unchanging pure awareness, which underlies the whole of life and death. In the stillness of meditation, we glimpse and return to that deep inner nature that we have so long ago lost sight of amid the busyness and distraction of our minds. . . . We are fragmented into so many different aspects. We don't know who we really are, or what aspects of ourselves we should identify or believe in. So many contradictory voices, dictates, and feelings fight for control over our inner lives that we find ourselves scattered everywhere, in all directions, leaving nobody at home. Meditation, then, is bringing the mind home.

Sogyal Rinpoche

When meditation works as it should, it will be a natural part of your being. There will no longer be anything apart from you to have faith in. . . . Only in this silence—the silence that lies behind thought—can one hear the symphony of the universe, can one hear the whisper of the Word, can one approach the inner temple wherein dwells the soul.

Ram Dass

When we raise ourselves through meditation to what unites us with the spirit, we quicken something within us that is eternal and unlimited by birth and death. Once we have experienced this eternal part in us, we can no longer doubt its existence. Meditation is thus the way to knowing and beholding the eternal, indestructible, essential center of our being.

Rudolf Steiner

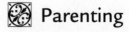 Parenting

There is a Spanish proverb that says "An ounce of parent is worth a pound of the clergy." While I'm not sure if the weights and measures are right, I am sure that parenting is a weighty job, an immeasurable responsibility. It is also a spiritual vocation, a calling just as clearly as being a member of the clergy is a calling, and just as challenging, even if the congregation is smaller! George F. Will writes that "we are given children to test us and make us more spiritual," for surely, as we guide our children, we strengthen our own spirituality as well.

Parenting, at its best, comes as naturally as laughter.
It is automatic, involuntary, unconditional love.

Sally James

The time will come in which the child will be looked upon as holy, even when the parents themselves have approached the mystery of life with profane feelings; a time in which all motherhood will be looked upon as holy, if it is caused by a deep emotion of love, and if it has called forth deep feelings of duty.

Ellen Key

Parenthood is a partnership with God . . . you are working with the creator of the universe in shaping human character and determining destiny.

Ruth Vaughn

The most important seed I can sow in this life is my children, and the love and knowledge that I can bestow upon them and the help I can give them.

Steven Seagal

Certain is it that there is no kind of affection so purely angelic as of a father to a daughter. In love to our wives there is desire; to our sons, ambition; but to our daughters there is something which there are no words to express.

Joseph Addison

A son and his mother are godly.

Rochelle Owens

God could not be everywhere and therefore he made mothers.

Jewish proverb

Your children are not your children.
They are the sons and daughters of Life's longing for itself.
They come through you but not from you,
And though they are with you yet they belong not to you.

Kahlil Gibran

We can't form our children on our own concepts;
we must take them and love them as God gives them to us.

Johann Wolfgang von Goethe

Having a child is surely the most beautifully irrational act that
two people in love can commit.

Bill Cosby

If I had my life to live over, instead of wishing away nine months of
pregnancy, I'd have cherished every moment of my chance in life to
assist God in a miracle. I would have sat on my lawn with my children
and not worried about the grass stains. When the kids kissed me
impetuously, I would never have said, "Later. Now go get washed
up for supper."

Erma Bombeck

Suddenly she was here. And I was no longer pregnant;
I was a mother. I never believed in miracles before.

Ellen Greene

Think always that, having the child at your breast, and having it in
your arms, you have God's blessing there.

Elizabeth Clinton

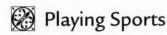 Playing Sports

I am not an athlete. However, one of the most spiritual experiences of my life came on an athletic field, on an ancient track in Greece, home of the Pythian Games, held once every four years in Delphi starting before the fifth century B.C., and the predecessor to the Olympics.

It was high summer and high noon and the heat was sweltering that day in Delphi, but some spirit took over when I caught the eye of Tracey, a fellow participant in the spiritual pilgrimage I was on. Without saying a word, we both assumed the position. "One, two, three!" another pilgrim yelled after catching on to our play, and we were off, racing down the ancient track.

To the Greeks, athletic competitions were religious rituals dedicated to the glorious gods who had created the body beautiful and powerful. Their competitions, like religious ceremonies, were replete with ritual, music, poetry, and art; they were full of passion, pageantry, piety, and praise. There was no concept of competition for competition's sake, but rather, the competition served to show the strength of the athlete's dedication to the gods. Spiritual seekers who are athletic would be well served—and would serve well—by adopting this ancient philosophy and bringing a religious attitude back to sports and competition.

I'm sure I lost the race that day, for I am not an athlete, but I ran for glory and I ran for the gods, and for the length of that track and the longer length of my memory, I became a body beautiful and a spirit powerful.

You have to be able to center yourself, to let all of your emotions go. . . .
Don't ever forget that you play with your soul as well as your body.

Kareem Abdul-Jabbar

Champions aren't made in the gyms. Champions are made from something they have deep inside them—a desire, a dream, a vision.

Muhammad Ali

By archery in the traditional sense, which he esteems as an art and honors as a national heritage, the Japanese does not understand a sport but, strange as this may sound at first, a religious ritual. And consequently, by the "art" of archery he does not mean the ability of the sportsman, which can be controlled, more or less, by bodily exercises, but an ability whose origin is to be sought in spiritual exercises and whose aim consists in hitting a spiritual goal, so that fundamentally the marksman aims at himself and may even succeed in hitting himself.

Eugen Herrigel

Golf is good for the soul.
You get so mad at yourself you forget to hate your enemies.

Will Rogers

All of us had flashes of this sense of oneness—making love, creating a work of art, when we're completely immersed in the moment, inseparable from what we're doing. This kind of experience happens all the time on the basketball floor.

Phil Jackson

Skiing is the next best thing to having wings.

Oprah Winfrey

I can sit in a ballpark after a game and love looking at the field. Everybody's gone, and the ballpark is empty, and I'll sit there. I sit there and think, "Is this as close to heaven as I'm going to get?" Or, "If I get to heaven, will there be baseball?"

Kim Braatz-Voisard

Baseball is religion without the mischief.

Thomas Boswell

It is most difficult, in my mind, to separate any success, whether it be in your profession, your family, or as in my case, in basketball, from religion.

John Wooden

Professional wrestling's most mysterious hold is on its audience.

Luke Neely

I'm fanatical about sport: there seems to me something almost religious about the fact that human beings can organise play, the spirit of play.

Simon Gray

 Praying

In the Islamic religion, there are five pillars upon which the pathway to God rests: One of them is prayer. There are five times a day specifically set aside for the practice: upon waking, at noon, in midafternoon, after sunset, and before sleep. Besides specific times to pray, there are specific ways to do so, including phrases uttered and prostrations repeated while facing toward Mecca. All these specifics, however, are only to serve the main intention of prayer as commanded in the Koran—to be in constant communication with the divine.

While the directions for prayer are specific, what is perhaps more interesting for non-Muslims is the content of Muslim prayers, which is universal. According to Huston Smith in his classic book *The Religions of Man,* there are two great themes to Muslim prayer: praise and gratitude, and supplication.

Supplication does not mean asking for things or favors (please let me win the lottery, please get me that promotion), but rather, asking for qualities (please make one more loving, more devout, more worthy of grace and mercy).

Prayer—however, whenever, wherever practiced—is clearly a way to connect with spirit. Much of the collected wisdom on prayer supports the Muslim belief that the most important contents of our prayers are praise, gratitude, and supplication, and that the specifics are only there to support the intent, which is to be in constant contact with the divine.

Prayer is simply a two-way conversation between you and God.

Billy Graham

Everyone prays in their own language, and there is no language that God does not understand.

Duke Ellington

Prayer is not asking. It is a longing of the soul.

Gandhi

Prayer is a very wide term. It includes all sorts of things, so my prayer life includes a great variety of activities: I may chant songs, go for a walk, soak in a hot tub, read poetry, or play with my cat. The essence of prayer as I understand the term is communication with the Ultimate. I think that prayer occurs whenever someone feels, "When I do this, then I really feel as if I'm at home with the Ultimate." That's a person's starting point for developing their prayer life. That could occur from watering African violets, reading sacred scripture, playing an instrument, or any number of activities.

David Steindl-Rast

Prayer makes your heart bigger, until it is capable of
containing the gift of God Himself.

Mother Teresa

That prayer has great power which a person makes with all his might.
It makes a sour heart sweet, a sad heart merry, a poor heart rich, a
foolish heart wise, a timid heart brave, a sick heart well, a blind heart
full of sight, a cold heart ardent. It draws down the great God into the
little heart; it drives the hungry soul up into the fullness of God; it
brings together two lovers, God and the soul, in a wondrous place
where they speak much of love.

Mechthild of Magdeburg

Personal prayer, it seems to me, is one of the simplest necessities of life,
as basic to the individual as sunshine, food, and water—and at times,
of course, more so. By prayer I mean an effort to get in touch with the
Infinite. We know that our prayers are imperfect. Of course they are.
We are imperfect human beings. A thousand experiences have
convinced me beyond room of doubt that prayer multiplies the
strength of the individual and brings within the scope of his
capabilities almost any conceivable objective.

Dwight D. Eisenhower

The purpose of daily prayer is the cultivation of a sense of the sacred.
Sacred energy renews us. Lives with no more sense of spiritual meaning
than that provided by shopping malls, ordinary television, and stagnant
workplaces are barren lives indeed. Spirituality enriches culture. Prayer
enables us to transform the world, because it transforms us.

Marianne Williamson

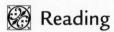 Reading

The connection between reading and worship is clear; one need only think of books such as the Bhagavad Gita, the Koran, the I Ching, the Bible, the Torah, the Dhammapada, and the Tao-te Ching to make that point. The Bible makes it even clearer, stating, "In the beginning was the Word; and the Word was with God and the Word was God." Reading spiritual texts is an obvious way of coming closer to God or to one's faith tradition, but reading in general can also enrich the spirit; as Anne Lamott says, it can "deepen and widen and expand our sense of life" and "feed the soul." Whether we read for worship, for pleasure, for illumination, for education, for understanding, or for any combination thereof, we become engaged for a period of time with what James Michener calls "the swirl and swing of words as they tangle with human emotion." For those who love reading, it is more than just an escape from life: It is life itself, folded up in the pages of a book, waiting for us to live and perhaps relive it. As Ruth Rendell confesses, "Some say life is the thing, but I prefer reading."

When we write books, make them, sell them, and read them, we're engaged in a process that has its own deep mystery. . . . Turning to the first page of any book is a ritual act, like going through the door of a cathedral or walking into a concert hall.

Thomas Moore

Books are companions, teachers, magicians, bankers of the treasures of the mind. Books are humanity in print.

Barbara W. Tuchman

In books lies the soul of the whole past time.

Thomas Carlyle

In reading holy books we receive many lights and divine calls. St. Jerome says that when we pray we speak to God; but when we read, God speaks to us. St. Ambrose says the same: "We address him when we pray; we hear him when we read." In prayer, God hears our petitions, but in reading we listen to his voice. We cannot, as I have already said, always have at hand a spiritual Father, nor can we hear the sermons of sacred orators, to direct and give us light to walk well in the way of God. Good books supply the place of sermons. St. Augustine writes that good books are, as it were, so many letters of love the Lord sends us; in them he warns us of our dangers, teaches us the way of salvation, animates us to suffer adversity, enlightens us, and inflames us with divine love. Whoever, then, desires to be saved and to acquire divine love, should often read these letters of paradise.

Saint Alphonsus de Liguori

Literature is where I go to explore the highest and lowest places in human society and in the human spirit, where I hope to find not absolute truth but the truth of the tale, of the imagination and of the heart.

Salman Rushdie

Every man who knows how to read has it in his power to magnify himself, to multiply the ways in which he exists, to make his life full, significant, and interesting.

Aldous Huxley

In a very real sense, people who have read good literature have lived more than people who cannot or will not read. . . . It is not true that we have only one life to live; if we can read, we can live as many more lives and as many kinds of lives as we wish.

S. I. Hayakawa

A room without books is like a body without soul.

Cicero

All books are variations on the books of wisdom we find in traditional religions, or the books that record our deeds on earth, or the book of our days. In some traditions, the story is told how as each person is born, the days of her life are written on a leaf that falls from the great Tree of Life. Beneath and beyond the facts and information offered in a book lies its mystery, its echo of sacred books, and it is in this hidden resonance that the book finds its enchantment. The heavenly book held so reverently in the hands of angels can be seen in any book, provided you have the eyes for it.

Thomas Moore

 # Sleeping

As a child, I was taught, like so many other children, to say a prayer at night that began, "Now I lay me down to sleep. I pray the Lord my soul to keep." While I knew my body lay peacefully in bed while I slept, I wondered where my soul flew off to, and marveled at the strangers and familiars it kept company with on its journeys. I understood the need to ask God to keep my soul, because those night-flights were both delightful and dangerous, mostly safe but sometimes unsound.

Sleeping is a both a natural and a powerful way of connecting with our spirituality. As we prepare to sleep, we gather our thoughts, we still our minds, we become reflective, and sometimes we talk to our souls or to our gods, and as we enter the twilight of sleep, we listen for replies. While we sleep, our bodies rest and rejuvenate while our souls travel on the wings of dreams and wild imaginings to worlds beyond our world, where, as D. H. Lawrence so wonderfully expressed, we are "dipped again in God, and new-created."

As an eagle, weary after soaring in the sky, folds its wings and flies down to rest in its nest, so does the shining Self enter the state of dreamless sleep, where one is freed from all desires.

Brihadaranyaka Upanishad

O bed! O bed! delicious bed!
That heaven upon earth to the weary head.

Thomas Hood

It is a delicious moment, certainly, that of being well-nestled in bed and feeling that you shall drop gently to sleep. The good is to come, not past; the limbs are tired enough to render the remaining in one posture delightful; the labor of the day is gone.

Leigh Hunt

Sleep is the most blessed and blessing of all natural graces.

Aldous Huxley

Thank God for sleep! And when you cannot sleep,
still thank Him that you live to lie awake.

John Oxenham

Sleep is the best meditation.

the Dalai Lama

In bed my real love has always been the sleep that rescued me
by allowing me to dream.

Luigi Pirandello

Have courage for the great sorrows of life and patience for the small
ones; when you have laboriously accomplished your daily task, go to
sleep in peace. God is awake.

Victor Hugo

There may be those on earth who dress better or eat better, but those
who enjoy the peace of God sleep better.

L. Thomas Holdcroft

A nap is not to be confused with sleeping. We sleep to recharge our
bodies. We nap to care for our souls. . . . The more naps you take, the
more awakenings you experience.

Sarah Ban Breathnach

My bed is the place where it all comes together. Here is where I think
naked thoughts, daydream, make love, worry, plot, argue, get my back
scratched, speculate, talk about growing old, and, finally, cut the
mooring ties and drift out with the dream tide. The bed, the place
where we are born and die, is our primeval place.

Laura Green

 Speaking

My niece and nephew were in the backseat of the car, arguing about something petty as siblings are prone to do. Hayley, around six at the time, made some snide comment to her brother, aimed at shutting down the conversation by proving her own superiority. It wasn't very nice.

Hayden, around four at the time, turned to her and replied with his own tone of superiority, "Hayley, God heard what you just said." To which she upped the ante of smugness by shooting back, "Hayden, God hears *everything.*"

Hayden turned from her and turned within. He literally shrank down in his car seat, and with his eyes shifting back and forth, he was quiet for a long moment as I waited, full of curiosity, for his retort.

It was simple, quiet, and intoned with guilt.

"Uh-oh."

I have often marveled at that response. I would have given anything to be inside his head at that moment. What possible transgressions could that angel of a little boy have already committed that would have him shrink down in his car seat in utter humility?

I remembered once a youth pastor of mine telling us that we should speak every word with the knowledge that God is listening. I was horrified at that thought, humbled like Hayden when I realized that God did not have selective hearing. I imagined his chagrin at some of the things I had let slip from my tongue lately, and I lamented loudly that no human being can be expected to speak virtuously all of the time. It might have helped me had my pastor shared that right speaking is one of the eight virtues of a boddhisatva, or saint, in the Buddhist tradition.

None of us—Hayden or myself or you included—is a saint yet, but all of us can practice the virtue of right speaking.

> Kind words can be short and easy to speak,
> but their echoes are truly endless.
>
> Mother Teresa

Before you speak, ask yourself:
Is it kind, is it necessary,
Is it true, does it improve on the silence?

Shirdi Sai Baba

I pray without ceasing now. My personal prayer is:
Make me an instrument which only truth can speak.

Peace Pilgrim

Speech is the embodiment of the unity between physical and spiritual.
It is the conduit for taking our earthly actions to a higher plane. . . . We
have a physical, earthly occurrence which is simultaneously a heavenly,
spiritually significant experience as well. When we have a convergence
of spiritual and physical, we must take note, and we do so by using this
very convergence that exists in our bodies—speech.

Rabbi Yehudah Prero

No man of wisdom can demonstrate his knowledge save by means of
words. . . . Moreover words and utterances should be both impressive
and penetrating. However, no word will be infused with these two
qualities unless it be uttered wholly for the sake of God and with
due regard for the exigencies of the occasion and the people.

Bahá'u'lláh

You can speak well if your tongue can
deliver the message of your heart.

John Ford

I do not speak of what I cannot praise.

Johann Wolfgang von Goethe

Speech is the mirror of the soul; as a man speaks, so he is.

Publilius Syrus

In positive terms, right speech means speaking in ways that are
trustworthy, harmonious, comforting, and worth taking to heart.
When you make a practice of these positive forms of right speech,
your words become a gift to others.

Thanissaro Bhikkhu

Language is a solemn thing: it grows out of life . . . out of its agonies
and ecstasies, its wants and weariness. Every language is a temple in
which the soul of those who speak it is enshrined.

Oliver Wendell Holmes

Your word is the power that you have to create. Your word is the gift
that comes directly from God. . . . The Bible, speaking of the creation
of the universe, says, "In the beginning there was the word, and the
word was with God, and the word is God." Through the word you
express your creative power. It is through the word that you manifest
everything. Regardless of what language you speak, your intent
manifests through the word. What you dream, what you feel, and
what you really are, all will be manifested through your word.

Don Miguel Ruiz

Studying Religions

The Dalai Lama has spoken out time and time again on the importance of studying other religions. He says, "I believe the purpose of all the major religious traditions is not to construct big temples on the outside, but to create temples of goodness and compassion *inside,* in our hearts. Every major religion has the potential to create this. The greater our awareness is regarding the value and effectiveness of other religious traditions, then the deeper will be our respect and reverence toward other religions. This is the proper way for us to promote genuine compassion and a spirit of harmony among the religions of the world."

Studying other religious traditions is important, he believes, not only so we can understand each other and create harmony in our world, but also because human beings are diverse, and "one religion simply cannot satisfy the needs of such a variety of people." Having a broad knowledge of other religions affords us the opportunity to find the religion, or religions, best suited to our different dispositions. While the religion we were born into may not speak to us, another one practiced in another country or another culture or just around the corner might.

I suspect this is part of what's behind the current trend for so many of us to label ourselves "spiritual, not religious"—that we have taken what resonates with us from different religious traditions and mixed them together to form our own belief system, no longer recognizable as any distinct religion but certainly spiritual in nature. Perhaps George Bernard Shaw was right when he said, "There is only one religion, though there are a hundred versions of it." It is up to us to find, or create, our own version of it.

I take the assumption that every religion has been rooted in some mystical or transcendent experience. From that assumption, I just look at all the different systems as metaphors or doorways to God.

Ram Dass

I love you my brother whoever you are, whether you worship in your church, kneel in your temple, or pray in your mosque. You and I are all children of one faith, for the diverse paths of religion are fingers of the loving hand of one Supreme Being, a hand extended to all, offering completeness of spirit to all, eager to receive all.

Kahlil Gibran

No man is born to any religion; he has a religion in his own soul.

Swami Vivekananda

I go into the Muslim mosque and the Jewish synagogue and the Christian church and I see one altar.

Rumi

People are of different spiritual temperaments, and therefore will approach God in different ways.

Huston Smith

I find the world's religions really nourish me. I don't get caught up in the politics and the personality of a particular religion. It's the essence of the religions that matter, and when you remove the veneer like the language, they all basically speak about the same thing.

Bruce Davis

In the matter of religion, people eagerly fasten their eyes on the difference between their own creed and yours; whilst the charm of the study is in finding the agreements and identities in all the religions of humanity.

Ralph Waldo Emerson

God is universal, confined to no spot, defined by no dogma,
appropriated by no sect.

Mary Baker Eddy

A friendly study of the world's religions is a sacred duty.

Gandhi

Religion is probably, after sex, the second oldest resource which
human beings have available to them for blowing their minds.

Susan Sontag

And yet we are incurably religious. There is an inner restlessness
in us that is never full satisfied until we find God.

Eric Butterworth

 Teaching

How do we talk about teaching as a spiritual path when there are so many
different kinds of teachers? Jesus was a teacher, Buddha was a teacher,
preachers are teachers, people who lead New Age workshops are teachers—
it's clear how their teaching is a spiritual path. So what do they have in
common with the "unwashed masses," those who teach to captive crowds
high school Spanish or physical education or elementary school music or
college algebra?

The answer is that regardless of the subject matter or the willingness
of the student, any teacher can teach to the spirit—not just the mind—of
the student, to see the student as a spiritual being and not just an intellectual one—and in that case, we are all, Buddha and Ms. Brown alike, spiritual teachers. However, there's another answer, a more difficult truth.

I've taught to those captive crowds for fifteen years, and I can testify that what makes teaching a perfect path for spiritual seekers is that it is a path strewn with tests. Students complain of being tested too much, but try being a teacher, where you're tested every day! Jonathan Robinson explains how: "Unlike what I expected, being a teacher is a humbling experience. My goal is to be a pure servant who can help guide my students forward. Yet I frequently see that I fall short of what I'm being called to do. Even little transgressions, such as giving feedback to students while slightly annoyed at them, stands out like a big black dot against a perfectly white wall. From such moments, I see how far I have to go, and how big of a task I've taken on. However, that is the way of growth. There can be no great success in life without first enduring a thousand small failures. As a student and as a teacher, I've learned that when I face challenges bigger than I think I can handle, grace and growth inevitably result."

Grace, growth, and a dose of humility—three of the gifts of any spiritual path, including that of the teacher.

And I should say that teaching is all one thing, whatever the subject, however diverse the students. It is based on an act of generosity—the giving of self for the good of others, and is in no sense a mere hired function for which there is adequate remuneration. . . . [It is] a ministration which is necessary to society but for which there is no adequate measure. As teachers, we are all too aware that we do not always live up to our calling; but despite any shortcomings we should be unreserved in considering that calling noble almost beyond compare.

Louise Cowan

A word as to the education of the heart. We don't believe that this can be imparted through books; it can only be imparted through the loving touch of the teacher.

Cesar Chavez

The spiritual teacher fills in for your higher self until it awakens. The teacher observes you with compassionate acceptance. This attitude of the personal spiritual teacher creates an echo in your subtle inner beingness and, after a time, you begin to perceive your ego-self with the same compassionate acceptance and understanding as the spiritual teacher does. You are transformed.

Harry Palmer

An understanding heart is everything in a teacher, and cannot be esteemed highly enough. One looks back with appreciation to the brilliant teachers, but with gratitude to those who touched our human feeling. The curriculum is so much necessary raw material, but warmth is the vital element for the growing plant and for the soul of the child.

Carl Jung

There is no real teacher who in practice does not believe in the existence of the soul, or in a magic that acts on it through speech.

Allan Bloom

Teaching is the greatest act of optimism.

Colleen Wilcox

A teacher affects eternity; he can never tell where his influence stops.

Henry Adams

Whoever touches the life of the child touches the most sensitive point of a whole which has roots in the most distant past and climbs toward the infinite future.

Maria Montessori

Teaching is not always about passing on what you know,
it is about passing on who you are.

Julia Loggins

Traveling

I've been traveling and I've joined tours and I've taken journeys and I've set out on adventures and I've gone on vacations and I've undertaken pilgrimages. My particular intentions for the trip help define the term I'll use: I travel to explore, I tour to broaden my horizons, I journey to learn something, I take adventures to have fun, I go on vacation to relax and commune with my family or friends or nature, and I undertake pilgrimages to deepen my spirituality. However, what binds all of those trips and all these terms together is that every time I visit a new place, I am transformed by that place. Pierre Loti says it much more eloquently: "I have traveled around the world, changing my changing soul."

In her book *The Singular Pilgrim,* Rosemary Mahoney makes the observation, "The self can certainly be transformed by a physical journey," and then goes on to ask, "but in what way would it be changed by a physical journey with a spiritual intent?" What if we undertook all of our travels this way? What if we didn't save spiritual intent for pilgrimages to sacred sites but instead saw every journey as a chance to deepen our spirituality, and every place we travel to as a sacred site?

Lord, make me see thy glory in every place.

Michelangelo

A traveler am I and a navigator, and every day
I discover a new region within my soul.

Kahlil Gibran

I think that wherever your journey takes you, there are new gods waiting there, with divine patience—and laughter.

Susan M. Watkins

He who leaveth home in search of knowledge walketh in the path of God.

Mohammed

On my first trip to Italy, I found myself in Rome in heavy traffic, riding out the highway that leads to Florence. We were driving during the rush hour in winter, and so the sun was setting, and the unique pastel colors of the eternal city made the old buildings come alive in the warming light. Suddenly I had the sensation that I had been on that street before and that I was recognizing those buildings and their extraordinary colors. For just a few seconds, on that particular unfamiliar street and for the duration of those few blocks, I felt exquisitely and enchantingly at home. Such enchanted moments can feed the soul for a lifetime.

Thomas Moore

If we are always arriving and departing, it is also true that we are eternally anchored. One's destination is never a place but rather a new way of looking at things.

Henry Miller

What gives value to travel is fear . . . There is no pleasure in traveling, and I look upon it more as an occasion for spiritual testing.

Albert Camus

To travel is to take a journey into yourself.

Dena Kaye

[One way] of working toward harmony among the world's religions is for people of different religious traditions to go on pilgrimages together to visit one another's holy places. A few years ago, I started doing this practice myself in India. Since then, I have had the opportunity to travel as a pilgrim to Lourdes, the holy place in France, and to Jerusalem. In these places, I prayed with the followers of the various religions, sometimes in silent meditation. And in this prayer and meditation, I felt a genuine spiritual experience.

the Dalai Lama

Spirit of place! It is for this we travel, to surprise its subtlety; and where it is a strong and dominant angel, that place, seen once, abides entire in the memory with all its own accidents, its habits, its breath, its name.

Alice Meynell

Visioning and Dreaming

Napoleon Hill once wrote something that has always captivated me. "Cherish your visions and your dreams as they are the children of your soul; the blue prints of your ultimate achievements."

What if we really treated our visions and dreams like they were children of our souls? Like our children, we would know that we had a part in creating them, but we would also see them as children of God and treat them as the divine creatures they are. We would devote to our dreams our time; we would devote to our visions our attention; we would devote to them both our support and the best of our intentions. We would not judge them, but would love them unconditionally and watch them with wonder and joy. We would attend to their wants and needs; we would listen to them carefully; we would give them time to go outside and play. If they became unruly, we would gently straighten them out without squelching their spirits. With equal mixtures of patience and passion, we would engage the entirety of our spirit in transforming our dreams and visions from castles in the sky to heaven on earth.

Wishing is good for us. Daydreams, fantasies, castles in the air, and aspirations all drive us forward, impel us to make things happen. They also tell us a lot about ourselves. Our wishes come straight from our core, and they are loaded with vital information about who we are and who we can become. Keeping track of our wishes helps us tap into the energy that propels us to go after our happiness.

Barbara Ann Kipfer

I prefer to be a dreamer among the humblest, with visions to be realized, than lord among those without dreams and desires.

Kahlil Gibran

To come to be you must have a vision of Being, a Dream, a Purpose, a Principle. You will become what your vision is.

Peter Nivio Zarlenga

No heart has ever suffered when it goes in search of its dreams, because every second of the search is a second's encounter with God and eternity.

Paulo Coelho

The dreamers are the saviors of the world. As the visible world is sustained by the invisible, so men, through all their trials and sins and sordid vocations, are nourished by the beautiful visions of their solitary dreamers.

James Allen

Dreams pass into the reality of action. From the action stems the dream again; and this interdependence produces the highest form of living.

Anaïs Nin

We grow great by dreams. All big men are dreamers. They see things in the soft haze of a spring day or in the red fire of a long winter's evening. Some of us let these great dreams die, but others nourish and protect them; nurse them through bad days till they bring them to the sunshine and light which comes always to those who sincerely hope that their dreams will come true.

Woodrow Wilson

The moment of enlightenment is when a person's dreams of possibilities become images of probabilities.

Vic Braden

A man's dreams are an index to his greatness.

Zadok Rabinowitz

We are the music makers. We are the dreamers of the dreams.

Arthur O'Shaughnessy

 Walking

There is a form of meditation in Buddhism called "walking meditation." As Thich Nhat Hanh explains, "In Buddhism, there is a word which means wishlessness or aimlessness. The idea is that we do not put anything ahead of ourselves and run after it. When we practice walking meditation, we walk in this spirit. We just enjoy the walking, with no particular aim or destination. Our walking is not a means to an end. We walk just for the sake of walking."

One of the goals of walking meditation is to cultivate awareness of the body, leading to an experience of peace. Hanh explains, "Breathing in, one step, breathing out, the other step—keeping awareness of our breathing and the movement of our feet. When we practice this way, we feel deeply at ease, and our problems and anxieties drop away, and peace and joy fill our hearts."

A second goal is to cultivate awareness of the body of the Earth, which Hanh says can also lead to an experience of peace. "Walking mindfully on the Earth can restore our peace and harmony, and it can restore the Earth's peace and harmony as well. . . . When we practice walking meditation, we massage the Earth with our feet and plant seeds of joy and happiness with each step." I like imagining walking in that way, as not only good for my body and mind, but good for the Earth itself—now there's one woman who deserves a good massage!

Aldous Huxley said, "My father considered a walk among the mountains as the equivalent of churchgoing." For those of us thinking outside the church in seeking the spiritual, it may be as simple as stepping outside and taking a walk.

If you are seeking creative ideas, go out walking.
Angels whisper to a man when he goes for a walk.

Raymond Inmon

When you walk across the fields with your mind pure and holy, then from all the stones, and all growing things, and all animals, the sparks of their soul come out and cling to you, and then they are purified and become a holy fire in you.

Hasidic saying

It is not talking but walking that will bring us to heaven.

Matthew Henry

Give me the strength to walk the soft earth, a relative to all that is!

Black Elk

Reading about nature is fine, but if a person walks in the woods and listens carefully, he can learn more than what is in books, for they speak with the voice of God.

George Washington Carver

All truly great thoughts are conceived by walking.

Friedrich Nietzsche

In beauty may I walk.
All day long may I walk.
Through the returning seasons may I walk.
On the trail marked with pollen may I walk.
With grasshoppers about my feet may I walk.
With dew about my feet may I walk.
With beauty may I walk.
With beauty before me, may I walk.
With beauty behind me, may I walk.
With beauty above me, may I walk.
With beauty below me, may I walk.
With beauty all around me, may I walk.
In old age wandering on a trail of beauty, lively, may I walk.
In old age wandering on a trail of beauty, living again, may I walk.
It is finished in beauty.
It is finished in beauty.

a Navajo prayer

Walking is the great adventure, the first meditation, a practice of
heartiness and soul primary to humankind. Walking is the exact
balance between spirit and humility.

Gary Snyder

Walking uplifts the spirit. Breathe out the poisons of tension, stress,
and worry; breathe in the power of God. Send forth little silent prayers
of goodwill toward those you meet. Walk with a sense of being a part
of a vast universe. Consider the thousands of miles of earth beneath
your feet; think of the limitless expanse of space above your head.
Walk in awe, wonder, and humility.

Wilferd A. Peterson

 # Working

I love the way Marianne Williamson envisions work. In her book *A Return
to Love,* she writes, "No matter what we do, we can make it our ministry.
No matter what form our job or activity takes, the content is the same as
everyone else's: we are here to minister to human hearts. If we talk to
anyone, or see anyone, or even think of anyone, then we have the opportunity to bring more love into the universe." It doesn't matter whether we
are a waiter, a salesclerk, a teacher, a police officer—we are all here to
minister, which in its broadest definition simply means to tend to
someone's wants and needs. Seen in this way, there is no work that is
more important than any other work, for all work done in the right spirit
is ministerial.

What if we dropped the words *work* or *job* from our vocabulary when
it comes to our professions and used the word *ministry* instead? What if
we kissed our beloved in the morning and said, "Good-bye, honey. I'm
off to my ministry now"? What if instead of asking someone, "Where do

you work?" we asked, "Where do you do your ministry?" Redefining work in this way would mean that for most of us, for at least eight hours a day, at least forty hours a week, we would be in touch with spirit as we minister to the spirit within others.

No work is secular. All work is adoration and worship.

Swami Vivekananda

There is always the danger that we may just do the work for the sake of the work. This is where the respect and the love and the devotion come in—that we do it to God, to Christ, and that's why we try to do it as beautifully as possible.

Mother Teresa

The decision as to what your career is to be is a very deep and important one, and it has to do with something like a spiritual requirement and commitment.

Joseph Campbell

The shop, the barn, the scullery, and the smithy become temples when men and women do all to the glory of God! The "divine service" is not a thing of a few hours and a few places, but all life becomes holiness unto the Lord, and every place and thing, as consecrated as the tabernacle and its golden candlestick.

C. H. Spurgeon

Occupation was one of the pleasures of paradise, and we cannot be happy without it.

Anna Brownell Jameson

When you spend your life doing what you love to do, you are nourishing your Soul. It matters not what you do, only that you love whatever you happen to do. Some of the happiest people I've known have been nannies, gardeners, and housekeepers. They put their hearts into their work, and they used the work itself as a vehicle to nourish their Souls. I've known other people with more prestigious professions who absolutely hated their jobs. What good is it to be a doctor or a professional if you do not genuinely love what you do? Working in a job you do not love does nothing to nourish your Soul.

Work nourishes the soul. All the creatures of the universe are busy doing work, and we honor life when we work. The type of work is not important: the fact of the work is. All work feeds the soul if it is honest and done to the best of our abilities and if it brings joy to others.

Elisabeth Kübler-Ross

Our work is meant to be a grace. It is a blessing and a gift, even a surprise and an act of unconditional love, toward the community— and not just the present community that may or may not compensate us for our work, but the community to come, the generations that follow our work.

Matthew Fox

Orare est laborare, laborare est orare.
To pray is to work, to work is to pray.

Benedictine order motto

 Worshipping

The church is often referred to as "a house of worship." When we think outside the church, we think of the entire world as a house of worship. The word *cloister* is synonymous with a religious residence, so when Joanna Macy wrote, "The world is our cloister," she means to have us see the entire world as our religious residence where all of our actions can be seen as religious, can be called worship. Kahlil Gibran wrote,

> He to whom worshipping is a window,
> to open but also to shut, has not
> yet visited the house of his soul whose
> windows are open from dawn to dawn.

True worship takes place from dawn to dawn, from Sunday to Sunday, from inside here to outside there, without beginning or end. We constantly observe what we are doing and ask ourselves, How is this worship? And whom or what am I worshipping? and if the answers are not agreeable to our souls, we change ourselves or change the service.

A person will worship something, have no doubt about that.
We may think our tribute is paid in secret in the dark recesses of our hearts, but it will out. That which dominates our imaginations and our thoughts will determine our lives, and our character. Therefore, it behooves us to be careful what we worship, for what we are worshipping we are becoming.

Ralph Waldo Emerson

The instinct to worship is hardly less strong than the instinct to eat.

Dorothy Thompson

I daresay anything can be made holy by being sincerely worshipped.

Iris Murdoch

Worship is transcendent wonder.

Thomas Carlyle

It is only when men begin to worship that they begin to grow.

Calvin Coolidge

Divine worship is as natural for men almost as neighing
is for horses or barking for dogs.

Marsilio Ficino

Later, in my trips to Nepal and Bali, I encountered worship that was
totally open and free. Children play on the religious monuments.
In Bali, there's no word for religion or art because it's all part of what
you do; it's not separate from life. The Balinese sense of integration
made sense to me. Seeing a non-pompous way of worshiping
definitely had an impact on me.

Emmett Miller

Worship is the highest act of which a person is capable. It not only
stretches us beyond all the limits of our finite selves to affirm the
divine depth of mystery and holiness in the living and eternal God,
but it opens us at the deepest level of our being to an act which
unites us most realistically with our fellow man.

Samuel H. Miller

Unless men see a beauty and delight in the worship of God,
they will not do it willingly.

John Owen

The act of divine worship is the inestimable privilege of man, the
only created being who bows in humility and adoration.

Hosea Ballou

An evolved soul is always a worshipper of God, one who worships
God in everything, for God is *in* everything.

Ernest Holmes

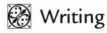 # Writing

A Chinese priest, when advising his followers in a better understanding of the complexity of the Buddhist scriptures, offered this: "If you do not understand, write the sutra. Then you will see its inner meaning." In this advice, he was stating what all teachers know—that there is a powerful link between learning and writing.

Popular spiritual writer Thomas Moore writes of his personal experience with the connection between writing and learning: "The art of writing can be a means by which you learn lessons in the spiritual life. For my part, when people ask me what meditation practices I pursue, I feel at a loss because I know they hope that I have studied with a teacher from India or Tibet and that I have much ceremony and tradition around my practice. The fact is that I consider my primary contemplative exercise to be my writing, my daily work of putting words on a page and even enjoying the playfulness and graphic capacities of my computer. For me, play, work, and spiritual practice come together in the activity by which I make my daily bread."

Writing doesn't have to be your bread-and-butter occupation, of course, to play a part in your spiritual formation. Writing in a journal for only a readership of yourself or your god is just as powerful. For people for whom even that type of writing is uncomfortable or unnatural, you can take a tip from the monks in the centuries before the printing press or from the Chinese priest above by finding a sacred passage that speaks to you and copying it in your own handwriting: a powerful way of learning spiritual lessons and imprinting upon your soul sacred thought.

I am writing this [my journal] for myself because paper plays a definite part in the spiritual formation of a writer. I am a writer, because for me to write is to think and to live and also in some degree even to pray.

Thomas Merton

It is necessary to write, if the days are not to slip emptily by. How else, indeed, to clap the net over the butterfly of the moment? For the moment passes, it is forgotten; the mood is gone; life itself is gone. That is where the writer scores over his fellows: He catches the changes of his mind on the hop. Growth is exciting; growth is dynamic and alarming. Growth of the soul, growth of the mind.

Vita Sackville-West

In writing poetry, all of one's attention is focused on some inner voice.

Li-Young Lee

The only time I know that something is true is the moment I discover it in the act of writing.

Jean Malaquais

Really, in the end, the only thing that can make you a writer is the person that you are, the intensity of your feeling, the honesty of your vision, the unsentimental acknowledgment of the endless interest of the life around and within you.

Santha Rama Rau

A writer is dear and necessary for us only in the measure of which he reveals to us the inner workings of his very soul.

Leo Tolstoy

I should write for the mere yearning and fondness I have for the beautiful, even if my night's labors should be burnt every morning and no eye shine upon them.

John Keats

The act of writing is the act of discovering what you believe.

David Hare

Writing is a form of therapy; sometimes I wonder how all those who do not write, compose, or paint can manage to escape the madness, the melancholia, the panic fear which is inherent in a human situation.

Graham Greene

Writing teaches us our mysteries.

Marie de L'Incarnation

EXPERIENCES

Men are wise in proportion, not to their experience,
but to their capacity for experience.

James Boswell

Where you are in consciousness has everything
to do with what you see in experience.

Eric Butterworth

Adversity and Suffering

The first of the Four Noble Truths of Buddhism is that all life is suffering. No one alive has failed to realize how much suffering there is in the world and ask themselves the question, "Why do we suffer?" and if we are religious, "Why does a loving God allow us to suffer?" There is one answer that emerges everywhere and thus appears to be a universal truth: that it is by suffering through adversity that we become more soulful. Poet John Keats summarized it by writing, "Do you not see how necessary a world of pains and troubles is to school an intelligence and make it a soul?"

It is often difficult to look at adversity this way, as a necessary gift to our souls, but it is precisely the fact that it *is* so difficult that makes it such a valuable spiritual attitude to refine. For me, the following nine words by Masahide help me to remember this attitude.

> Barn's burnt down—
> now
> I can see the moon.

When adversity strikes, when suffering ensues, when our barns burn down (and they will, and they will again), we can focus on the gift: a clear vision of the moon, whose reflected light can provide insight into our spiritual natures.

> It appears that when life is broken by tragedy
> God shines through the breach.
>
> George A. Buttrick

> There is in every heart a spark of heavenly fire
> which lies dormant in the broad daylight of prosperity,
> but which kindles up and beams
> and blazes in the dark hour of adversity.
>
> Washington Irving

It constantly happens that the Lord permits a soul to fall
so that it may grow humbler.

Teresa of Avila

The storms of life can be used for good in our lives if we
let them drive our spirits higher and closer to God.

Roy Lessin

Adversity in the things of this world opens the door
for spiritual salvation.

A. J. Toynbee

I thank God for my handicaps for, through them,
I have found myself, my work, and my God.

Helen Keller

Trials, temptations, disappointments—all these are helps instead of
hindrances, if one uses them rightly. They not only test the fiber of
character but strengthen it. Every conquering temptation represents
a new fund of moral energy. Every trial endured and weathered in the
right spirit makes a soul nobler and stronger than it was before.

James Buckham

Every hardship; every joy; every temptation is a challenge of the spirit;
that the human soul may prove itself. The great chain of necessity
wherewith we are bound has divine significance; and nothing
happens which has not some service in working out the sublime
destiny of the human soul.

Elias A. Ford

Adversity is the diamond dust Heaven polishes its jewels with.

Robert Leighton

I know God will not give me anything I can't handle.
I just wish that He didn't trust me so much.

Mother Teresa

All suffering prepares the soul for vision.

Martin Buber

Life has meaning only in the struggle. Triumph or defeat is in
the hands of the gods. So let us celebrate the struggle!

Swahili warrior song

 Aging

Dr. George E. Vaillant is the director of the Harvard Study of Adult Development and the author of a book called *Aging Well*. Of the connection between aging and spirituality, he writes, "in theory, spirituality should deepen in old age for all of us. For if growing older does not inevitably lead toward spiritual development, growing older does alter the conditions of life in ways that are conducive to spirituality. Aging slows us down and provides us time and peace to smell life's flowers. Aging simplifies our daily routine and facilitates the acceptance of the things we cannot change. Aging banks our instinctual fires and increases our capacity to be internally quiet. Aging compels us to contemplate death. . . . Aging focuses us toward becoming one with the ultimate ground of being." Perhaps this is why they are called the golden years, as we learn to focus on what is truly valuable and eternal.

The beauty of the wisdom of aging is that we don't have to wait until we have grown old to embody it, for our bodies are constantly aging, providing our spirits with vessels for growth as well.

To know how to grow old is the master-work of wisdom, and one of the most difficult chapters in the great art of living.

Henri Amiel

For inside all the weakness of old age, the spirit, God knows, is as mercurial as it ever was.

May Sarton

Old age is that night of life, as night is the old age of day. Still night is full of magnificence and, for many, it is more brilliant than the day.

Anne-Sophie Swetchine

When grace is joined with wrinkles, it is adorable. There is an unspeakable dawn in happy old age.

Victor Hugo

These are the soul's changes. I don't believe in aging. I believe in forever altering one's aspect to the sun. Hence my optimism.

Virginia Woolf

Beautiful young people are accidents of nature, but beautiful old people are works of art.

Eleanor Roosevelt

You can only perceive real beauty in a person as they get older.

Anouk Aimée

As a white candle
In a holy place,
So is the beauty
Of an aged face.

Joseph Campbell

If wrinkles must be written upon our brows, let them not be written upon the heart. The spirit should not grow old.

James A. Garfield

Like a morning dream, life becomes more and more bright the longer we live, and the reason of everything appears more clear. What has puzzled us before seems less mysterious, and the crooked paths look straighter as we approach the end.

Jean Paul Richter

For a younger person it is almost a sin—and certainly a danger—to be too much occupied with himself; but for the aging person it is a duty and a necessity to give serious attention to himself. After having lavished its light upon the world, the sun withdraws its rays in order to illumine itself.

Carl Jung

The golden age is before us, not behind us.

Saint Simon

I look forward to growing old and wise and audacious.

Glenda Jackson

You never grow old until you've lost all your marvels.

Merry Brown

 # Becoming

Swami Vivekananda was a nineteenth-century Indian monk who is often credited with being India's spiritual ambassador to the West due to his efforts to enrich the spiritual life of Americans through an introduction to Vendanta philosophy. One of the themes of Vendanta is the search for unity, whereby we seek the divine by becoming more divine ourselves; its ultimate realization is that we are always and already one with the divine. He explains, "Religion is realization; not talk, nor doctrine, nor theories however beautiful they may be. It is being and becoming, not hearing, or acknowledging; it is the whole soul becoming what it believes. That is religion."

In the West several decades ago, the catch-phrase for this work might have been *finding oneself;* now we might refer to it as *spiritual growth,* the process by which we fully realize our relationship with the divine spirit both within and without, and where we strive to achieve that famous Western mantra "to be all that we can be."

You are an evolving person. You have come out of all time and are going to all time, from glory to glory, led by an image of the Lord. There is a perfect image at the center to cause what you are. We don't have to manufacture goodness. . . . Just let it through.

Raymond Charles Barker

To be what we are, and to become what we are capable of becoming,
is the only end of life.

Baruch Spinoza

As human beings, our greatness lies not so much in being able to
remake the world . . . as in being able to remake ourselves.

Gandhi

My business is not to remake myself,
But to make the absolute best of what God made.

Robert Browning

Nothing ever is, everything is becoming.

Plato

The gift is that we are unfinished. The sixth day is not yet over for us.

Joanne Greenberg

I see life in terms of transformation: matter being transformed into
life, life into consciousness, consciousness into Divine Experience.

Bede Griffiths

The spiritual journey does not consist of arriving at a new destination
where a person gains what he did not have, or becomes what he is not.
It consists in the dissipation of one's own ignorance concerning oneself
and life, and the gradual growth of that understanding which begins
the spiritual awakening. The finding of God is a coming to one's self.

Aldous Huxley

Become aware of what is in you.
Announce it, pronounce it,
produce it, and give birth to it.

Meister Eckhart

One day, a woman found herself standing at Heaven's gate. The angels' only question to her was, "Zusai, why weren't you Zusai?" Within that simple question lies the heart of all our soul work. If you are David, why aren't you fully David? If you are Susan, why aren't you completely Susan? We are here on Earth to become who we are meant to be.

Angeles Arrien

We all have some power in us that knows its own ends. It is that that drives us on to what we must finally become. We have only to conceive of the possibility and somehow the spirit works in us to make it actual. This is the true meaning of transformation. This is the real metamorphosis. Our further selves are contained within us, as the leaves and blossoms are in the tree. We have only to find the spring and release it.

David Malouf

Believing

I struggled in writing this book with whether to separate belief and faith into two separate categories. Were they fundamentally that different? In what ways?

Whenever I asked questions like this as a child, my grandfather always sent me to the dictionary. When he died, I asked to have that dictionary, the faded red Webster's he and I used to consult. I looked up the difference between those two words now, upon hearing his voice in my head suggesting I do so. There, faith is defined as "unquestioning belief" and belief is defined as "conviction that certain things are true; faith, especially religious faith." In the inimitable way that only dictionaries can do, I am spun in circles, one definition leading to the other leading back to the first.

Still, I believe (or, perhaps I have faith?) that there is a distinction between the two. And then I find it in a quote by Joseph Fort Newton: "Belief is truth held in the mind; faith is a fire in the heart." Setting aside my analytical nature in favor of a poetic metaphor, I stop the struggling and spinning over absolute distinction and with faith, offer up the experience of believing as important to our spiritual development.

You're not free until you've been made captive by supreme belief.

Marianne Moore

I believe that in our constant search for security we can never gain any peace of mind until we secure our own soul. And this I do believe above all, especially in my times of greatest discouragement, that I must believe—that I must believe in my fellow people—that I must believe in myself—that I must believe in God—if life is to have any meaning.

Margaret Chase Smith

If thou canst believe, all things are possible to him that believeth.

Mark 9:23

Man makes holy what he believes.

Ernest Renan

It is better to believe than to disbelieve, in so doing you bring everything to the realm of possibility.

Albert Einstein

Man is a being born to believe. And if no church comes forward with its title-deeds of truth to guide him, he will find altars and idols in his own heart and his own imagination.

Benjamin Disraeli

Every believer is God's miracle.

Philip James Bail

I believe in the sun even when it isn't shining. I believe in love even when I am alone. I believe in God even when He is silent.

World War II refugee

You have to believe in gods to see them.

Hopi saying

If you wish to strive for peace of soul and pleasure, then believe.

Heinrich Heine

 Chaos

A friend of mine called the other night in tears. Everything was in upheaval, and she felt like she was trying to piece together the puzzle of her life to make a coherent picture without knowing what the picture was supposed to look like or if she even had all the pieces she needed.

Chaos.

I've seen her in this place before, and I don't worry about her there. She is a woman in touch with soul; she is a woman who listens to spirit.

Her tears were her ego releasing its need to know, its need for order, its needs for answers *now*. For she knows that "Chaos is the soul of creation. It plows the ground of intuition. Without chaos, nothing will grow" (Michele Cassou).

Chaos is defined as "the gaping void out of which comes creation; not knowing." When my friend called that night, she cried tears that fell into the gaping void, but I don't worry about her there: I know that her tears of not knowing will water the ground from which will spring the answers that will soothe her soul and make sense of her life, as long as she listens to her spirit.

Chaos. The soul of creation.

Before anything is brought back into order, it is quite normal for it to be brought first into a kind of confusion, a virtual chaos. In this way, things that fit together badly are severed from each other; and when they have been severed, then the Lord arranges them in order.

Emanuel Swedenborg

Odd how the creative power at once brings the whole universe to order.

Virginia Woolf

Oh, God, why don't I remember that a little chaos is good for the soul?

Marilyn French

The splendid discontent of God
With chaos made the world.

Ella Wheeler Wilcox

In all chaos there is a cosmos, in all disorder a secret order.

Carl Jung

It is important to do what you don't know how to do. It is important to see your skills as keeping you from learning what is deepest and most mysterious. If you know how to focus, unfocus. If your tendency is to make sense out of chaos, start chaos.

Carlos Castenada

Before the beginning of great brilliance, there must be chaos. Before a brilliant person begins something great, they must look foolish in the crowd.

the I Ching

I have a great belief in the fact that whenever there is chaos, it creates wonderful thinking.
I consider chaos a gift.

Septima Poinsette Clark

All genius is a conquering of chaos and mystery.

Otto Weininger

I believe in deeply ordered chaos.

Francis Bacon

Nothing in the world can change from one reality into another unless it first turns into nothing, that is, into the reality of the between-stage. And then it is made into a new creature, from the egg to the chick. The moment when the egg is no more and the chick is not yet, is nothingness. This is the primal state which no one can grasp because it is a force which precedes creation. It is called chaos.

Hasidic Master

You need chaos in your soul to give birth to a dancing star.

Friedrich Nietzsche

We live in a rainbow of chaos.

Paul Cézanne

 Contemplating Eternity

The Human Being, like a bird of the sea,
emerged from the ocean of the soul.
Earth is not the final place of rest
for a bird born from the sea.

Rumi

To contemplate the life of the soul is to consider time and eternity. Where did we come from? When will we return? Where is the sea from which our souls emerged, and is time really as eternal as those proverbial grains of sand?

Thomas Moore writes, "The soul wants union not only with other persons but also with another dimension altogether, one we call eternal, immortal, mythic, or a host of other names." We want to return to the place of rest from which we came; we long in time to submerge ourselves again in the eternal sea. We have no proof of our immortality save our intuitions and intimations, but it is enough.

I existed from all eternity and, behold, I am here;
and I shall exist till the end of time,
for my being has no end.

Kahlil Gibran

All around I behold your Infinity: the power of your
Innumerable arms, the vision of your innumerable
Eyes, the words from your innumerable mouths,
And the fire of life of your innumerable bodies.
Nowhere do I see a beginning or middle or end
Of you, O God of all, O Great Infinity.

the Bhagavad Gita

A red-hot belief in eternal glory is probably the best antidote
to human panic that there is.

Phyllis Bottome

One cannot help but be in awe when he contemplates the mysteries
of eternity, of life, of the marvelous structure of reality.

Albert Einstein

If the doors of perception were cleansed.
Everything would appear to man as it is—infinite.

William Blake

The few little years we spend on earth are only the first scene
in a Divine Drama that extends into Eternity.

Edwin Markham

I believe that man will not merely endure; he will prevail. He is
immortal, not because he alone among the creatures has an
inexhaustible voice, but because he has a soul, a spirit capable
of kindness and compassion.

William Falconer

The human soul cannot be equated with the brain, consciousness, or behavior. The soul is the very breath of our vitality and the unfathomable source of our identity. It is not a problem to be solved, but rather our very life that needs food and nurturing. The best food for the soul is a mixture of love, beauty, and excursions out of time where we glimpse the eternal. . . . Eternity is the proper time frame of the soul, whose immortality is ever present and whose endurance knows no limitation.

Thomas Moore

I believe in the immortality of the soul because I have within me immortal longings.

Helen Keller

All men's souls are immortal, but the souls of the righteous are immortal and divine.

Socrates

In eternity there is indeed something true and sublime. But all these times and places and occasions are now and here. God himself culminates in the present moment and will never be more divine in the lapse of the ages. Time is but a stream I go a-fishing in. I drink at it, but when I drink I see the sandy bottom and detect how shallow it is. Its thin current slides away but eternity remains.

Henry David Thoreau

The created world is but a small parenthesis in eternity.

Sir Thomas Browne

 Desire

The Cloud of Unknowing, a fourteenth-century mystical text written by an unknown author, contains these words: "For it is not what you are or have been that God looks upon with merciful eyes, but what you long to be." In so many religious and spiritual traditions, longing and desire are seen as an evil, as an impediment on the path to the divine. But to condemn all desire seems to me simplistic. Surely it must depend on what you desire, why you desire it, and what you are willing—or not—to sacrifice for your desire. Surely desire can be spiritual, and can serve spirituality.

The Upanishads, the ancient Indian spiritual and poetic text, teach "You are what your deep driving desire is; as your deep driving desire is, so is your will; as your will is so is your deed; as your deed is so is your destiny." Thus, if we deeply desire spiritual connection, in whatever form that takes, whether in a love affair with a person, with a place, with our work, or with the Divine itself, that desire has the power to become our will, our deed, and our destiny.

Desires are the pulses of the soul; as physicians judge by the appetite, so may you by desires.

Thomas Manton

I believe that the desire to please You does in fact please You.
I hope I have that desire in everything I do.
I hope I never persist in anything apart from that desire.

Thomas Merton

There is one great truth on this planet: whoever you are, or whatever you do, when you really want something, it's because that desire originated in the soul of the universe. It's your mission on earth.

Paulo Coelho

Very few persons, comparatively, know how to Desire with sufficient intensity. They do not know what it is to feel and manifest that intense, eager, longing, craving, insistent, demanding, ravenous Desire which is akin to the persistent, insistent, ardent, overwhelming desire of the drowning man for a breath of air; of the shipwrecked or desert-lost man for a drink of water; of the famished man for bread and meat . . .

Robert Collier

To be with God is really to be involved with some enormous, over-whelming desire, and joy, and power which you cannot control, which controls you. I conceive of my own life as a journey toward something I did not understand, which in the going toward, makes me better.

James Baldwin

Limited in his nature, infinite in his desire,
man is a fallen god who remembers heaven.

Alphonse de Lamartine

The more wild and incredible your desire, the more willing and prompt God is in fulfilling it, if you will have it so.

Coventry Patmore

The desire is thy prayers; and if thy desire is without ceasing, thy prayer will also be without ceasing. The continuance of your longing is the continuance of your prayer.

Saint Augustine

The desire accomplished is sweet to the soul.

Proverbs 13:19

It is the soul's duty to be loyal to its own desires.
It must abandon itself to its master passion.

Rebecca West

Dreaming

Schopenhauer called this world "one great dream dreamed by a single Being, but in such a way that all the dream characters dream, too." This is echoed in the Cherokee saying that "there is but One Mind that underlies the dream," and echoed again by Thomas Mann, who wrote, "Now I know that it is not out of our single souls we dream. We dream anonymously and communally, if each after his own fashion. The great soul of which we are a part may dream through us, in our manner of dreaming, its own secret dreams, of its youth, its hope, its joy and peace—and its blood sacrifice."

It is an intriguing idea, that there is one Great Being dreaming, and we are the dreams that in turn dream too. It is an intriguing idea to imagine that we are tapping into that Great Soul while we dream, that it is dreaming through us its dreams. I've had dreams like that before, where I feel so connected to the universal spirit that I never want to wake up, dreams that feel like spiritual revelation and have so defined my spirituality that I will carry them with me the rest of my life. I am eager for those dreams that descend upon me like grace, and when my soul needs nourishment, I seek them and sometimes I find them, or perhaps they seek me and sometimes find me.

I've also had dreams where poodles stand on the side of the freeway holding helium balloons while Army trucks race by, proving that if the Great Being is the one dreaming, it also has one hell of a sense of humor!

Dream manfully and nobly, and thy dreams shall be prophets.

Edward G. Bulwer-Lytton

Our heart oft times wakes when we sleep, and God can speak to
that, either by words, by proverbs, by signs and similitudes,
as well as if one was awake.

John Bunyan

All human beings are also dream beings.
Dreaming ties all mankind together.

Jack Kerouac

Dreaming is an act of pure imagination, attesting in all men a
creative power, which, if it were available in waking, would
make every man a Dante or Shakespeare.

Francis Herbert Hedge

Dreams are self-luminous: they shine of themselves as gods do.
Myths are public dreams. Dreams are private myths. By finding
your own dream and following it through, it will lead you to
the myth world in which you live.

Joseph Campbell

Dreams are illustrations from the book your soul is writing about you.

Marsha Norman

A dream is a scripture, and many scriptures are nothing but dreams.

Umberto Eco

Dreams are sent by God.

Homer

The dream is the small hidden door in the deepest and most intimate sanctum of the soul, which opens into that primeval cosmic night that was soul long before there was a conscious ego and will be soul far beyond what a conscious ego could ever reach.

Carl Jung

A dream is a microscope through which we look at the hidden occurrences in our soul.

Erich Fromm

Dreams are . . . an expansion of life, an enlightenment, and a discipline. I thank God for my dream life; my daily life would be far poorer, if it wanted the second sight of dreams.

Amelia E. Barr

 # Dying

I handed my seven-year-old niece Hayley the small carton of milk and watched her examine it closely before drinking. "June 30, 2003," she announced.

"What's that?" I asked her.

"That's the milk's birthday," she matter-of-factly replied.

I smiled to myself, utterly charmed as always by what she knows, what she doesn't know, and what she only thinks she knows. "Actually," I said gently, "that's the day the milk dies."

I began wondering what it would be like if people, like milk, had an expiration date stamped on our cartons for everyone to read. And because I'm weird like this, I began musing about the difference between people and milk: that when people die, we have a sense that their death date is also their date of birth into a new life, but when milk dies . . .

You get the picture, absurd as it is. What I am trying to say is that maybe Hayley is right in her wrongness, that perhaps our expiration date is also our birth date, and that "death is birthing into another realm" (Terese Schroeder-Sheker), as most funerals acknowledge, as most religious and spiritual systems teach. Just like the carton is not the milk, so too, as David Brandt Berg notes, "your body is not the real you. It's just the physical house you live in. The real you is your spirit, which will live on forever." Thus, contemplating the enormity of death is contemplating the enormity of the spirit, which is one reason Buddha taught, "Of all footprints, that of the elephant is supreme. Similarly, of all mindfulness meditations, that on death is supreme."

For those who seek to understand it, death is a highly creative force. The highest *spiritual* values of life can originate from the thought and study of death.

Elisabeth Kübler-Ross

Dying is a wild night
and a new road.

Emily Dickinson

There is no death. Only a change of worlds.

Chief Seattle

Fear not death, for the sooner we die the longer we shall be immortal.

Benjamin Franklin

Is death the last sleep? No—it is the last and final awakening.

Sir Walter Scott

What we commonly call death does not destroy the body,
it only causes a separation of spirit and body.

Brigham Young

We never come fully to grips with life until we are willing
to wrestle with death.

James Hillman

Death is delightful. Death is dawn, the waking from a weary
night of fevers unto truth and light.

Joaquin Miller

Death only this mysterious truth unfolds,
The mighty soul, how small a body holds.

Juvenal

Death is the golden key that opens the palace of eternity.

John Milton

For what is it to die but to stand naked in the wind and to melt into the sun?

And what is it to cease breathing, but to free the breath from its restless tides, that it may rise and expand and seek God unencumbered?

Only when you drink from the river of silence shall you indeed sing.

And when you have reached the mountain top, then you shall begin to climb.

And when the earth shall claim your limbs, then shall you truly dance.

Kahlil Gibran

Enjoying Small Pleasures

Ludwig Mies Van Der Rohe once made an observation that is so simple, yet so wise, that I would venture to call it one of the most critical corner-stones of spiritual living. "God," he said, "is in the details."

I think of that quote when I closely examine the brushstrokes that created magic in Van Gogh's *Starry Night*. I think of that quote when I see the intricate markings resembling an owl's eye on the giant owl butterfly. I think of that quote when I look at the picture my nephew made for me when he was three. I've felt the grandeur of God when seeing the immensity of the Grand Canyon or the power of Niagara Falls or the ruins of the Acropolis, but it has struck me with equal and unparalleled intensity when I've looked carefully at the small, sweet juice-filled cells of an orange or listened closely to the lilting laughter of my lover. I cried while watching the bag-dancing-in-the-wind scene in the movie *American Beauty* (alone worth the cost of the ticket) because screenwriter Alan Ball got it right when he penned the words spoken by the troubled young man: "Sometimes there's so much beauty in the world I feel like I can't take it . . . and my heart is going to cave in."

> I am sitting here in the sun
> Watching the kittens playing
> And the children playing
> And I am convinced
> There is nothing worth doing more.
>
> Susan Fromberg Schaeffer

> God is in those details.
> I am doing something I learned early to do, I am
> paying attention to small beauties,
> whatever I have—as if it were our duty to
> find things to love, to bind ourselves to this world.
>
> Sharon Olds

The object of our lives is to look at, listen to, touch, taste things. Without them,—these sticks, stones, feathers, shells,—there is no Deity.

R. H. Blyth

My religion consists of a humble admiration of the illimitable spirit who reveals himself in the slight details we are able to perceive with our frail and feeble mind.

Albert Einstein

The invariable mark of wisdom is to see the miraculous in the common.

Ralph Waldo Emerson

Slipping
On my shoes,
Boiling water,
Toasting bread,
Buttering the sky;
That should be enough contact
With God in one day
To make anyone
Crazy.

Hafiz

Small kindnesses, small courtesies, small considerations, habitually practiced in our social intercourse, give a greater charm to the character than the display of great talents and accomplishments.

Mary Ann Kelty

It isn't the big pleasures that count the most;
it's making a great deal out of the little ones.

Jean Webster

Gifts and Talents

In schools across America, there are "Gifted and Talented" classes known as the GATE program. It greatly disturbs me to see these programs in school, for I fear the message that at least the name sends is that only a select few are gifted and talented, when it is a spiritual truth that we all are gifted and talented in our own ways. You will find that most of the quotes below express the same idea: that our gifts and talents come from God, and, therefore, it is incumbent upon us to give the gift back for the highest good.

But before we can use those gifts for *any* good, we have to believe they are there. Every child should be enrolled in a class called "Gifts and Talents" where they are encouraged and expected to find their gifts, and then create action plans for developing those talents and making use of them for the good of their own souls and the soul of the world.

God has given each of us gifts that we can express at work and home, not only in the church. But the gifts will not bring God glory unless it is expressed together with the character and attitudes of Jesus. Our gifts are given to reflect the God we serve.

Adeline Lim

This is how I define talent; it is a gift that God has given us in secret, which we reveal without knowing it.

Charles de Montesquieu

We all have many God-given gifts. The challenge with which we are each faced is to discover these gifts and then make full use of them by serving others. That is how our soul grows, in the highest sense: the soul stretches itself and fulfills its purpose.

John Gray

Neglect not the gift that is in thee.

1 Timothy 4:14

Since we have gifts that differ according to the grace given to us, each
of us is to exercise them accordingly: if prophecy, according to the
proportion of his faith; if service, in his serving; or he who teaches,
in his teaching; or he who exhorts, in his exhortation; he who gives,
with liberality; he who leads, with diligence; he who shows mercy,
with cheerfulness.

Romans 12:6–8

I believe that life is a journey, often difficult and sometimes incredibly
cruel, but we are well equipped for it if only we tap into our talents and
gifts and allow them to blossom.

Les Brown

God has given each of us our "marching orders." Our purpose here
on Earth is to find those orders and carry them out. Those orders
acknowledge our special gifts.

Søren Kierkegaard

When I stand before God at the end of my life, I would hope that
I would not have a single bit of talent left and could say, "I used
everything you gave me."

Erma Bombeck

Your talent is God's gift to you; what you do with it is your gift to God.

Leo Buscaglia

God doesn't give people talents that he doesn't want people to use.

Iron Eagle

All the talents of God are within you.
How could this be otherwise
When your soul
Derived from His
Genes!

Hafiz

 # Grace

My favorite definition of grace comes from Paul Tillich: "Accept the fact that you are accepted, despite the fact that you are unacceptable." Some of us have a hard time offering that kind of grace to others; some of us have a harder time offering it to ourselves. I am a perfectionist, my own worst enemy, and my own harshest judge. I laugh in recognition at Woody Allen's response in *Manhattan* to the statement "You think you're God." He replies, with deadpan seriousness, "I gotta model myself after someone." Yet Tillich's quote teaches me how to be full of grace toward myself, reminding me to accept myself despite sometimes feeling that I'm unacceptable.

This, after all, is what I've been taught that my role model would do.

Grace is also very important. Divine grace is there all around us.
Helpful beings and spirits are all around us. When our desire to be
in God's presence is really authentic, when we express that in our
thoughts (which are, in fact, prayers), then we get a great deal of
help. I think desire and intention are the two magic ingredients
for experiencing Grace.

Joan Borysenko

But grace means more than gifts. In grace something is transcended, once and for all overcome. Grace happens in spite of something; it happens in spite of separateness and alienation. Grace means that life is once again united with life, self is reconciled with self. Grace means accepting the abandoned one. Grace transforms fate into a meaningful vocation. It transforms guilt to trust and courage. The word *grace* has something triumphant in it.

Yrjö Kallinen

It was obedience which brought me grace, and after that experience I knew what God's grace was. One must be utterly abandoned to God; nothing matters but fulfilling His will.

Carl Jung

We're all stumbling towards the light with varying degrees of grace at any given moment.

Bo Lozoff

Grace is available for each of us every day—our spiritual daily bread—but we've got to remember to ask for it with a grateful heart and try not to worry about whether there will be enough for tomorrow. There will be.

Sarah Ban Breathnach

I move through my day-to-day life with a sense of appreciation and gratitude that comes from knowing how fortunate I truly am and how unearned all that I am thankful for really is. To have this perspective in my everyday consciousness is in itself a gift, for it leads to feeling "graced," or blessed, each time.

Jean Shinoda Bolen

I'm becoming more and more myself with time. I guess that's what grace is, the refinement of your soul through time.

Jewel

Nothing whatever pertaining to godliness and real holiness can be accomplished without grace.

Saint Augustine

The grace of God means something like: Here is your life. You might never have been, but you are because the party wouldn't have been complete without you. Here is the world. Beautiful and terrible things will happen. Don't be afraid. I am with you. Nothing can ever separate us. It's for you I created the universe. I love you. There's only one catch. Like any other gift, the gift of grace can be yours only if you'll reach out and take it. Maybe being able to reach out and take it is a gift too.

Frederick Buechner

You may try thousands of times, but nothing can be achieved without God's grace. One cannot see God without His grace. Is it an easy thing to receive grace? One must altogether renounce egotism; one cannot see God as long as one feels, "I am the doer." God doesn't easily appear in the heart of a man who feels himself to be his own master. But God can be seen the moment His grace descends.

Sri Ramakrishna

The One who is full of grace
Will find the ladder to the sky.

Rumi

 The Heart

One of my favorite books is a little treatise by depth psychologist James Hillman called *The Thought of the Heart and the Soul in the World*. In this book, Hillman argues that the heart is "the seat of the imagination," and thus it is of little wonder that when we speak of the heart, we speak in images, such as "a cold heart" and "a pure heart" and "a lonely heart"; we call people "heartbreakers" and "heartthrobs" and "heartless"; we speak of "a change of heart" and "wearing our hearts on our sleeves" and being "heartsick"; we advise people to "follow your heart" and "listen to your heart" and to "trust your heart," and on and on and on. Gail Godwin, in her book simply titled *Heart,* expands on Hillman's work, examining what the heart has meant to different cultures during different time periods, finding some very similar meanings and remarkably rich imaginings, particularly in religious and spiritual texts.

For the spiritual seeker, then, perhaps the heart of connecting with the divine lies in penetrating into the mystery of the heart; in other words, in "wholeheartedly" delving into "the heart of the matter," and doing so with "an open heart."

The way is not in the sky. The way is in the heart.

the Dhammapada

The heart is a sanctuary at the centre of which there is a little space, wherein the Great Spirit dwells, and this is the Eye. If the heart is not pure, the Great Spirit cannot be seen.

Black Elk

Our hearts are the wrapping, which preserve God's word; we need no more.

the Koran

The heart is deeper than rivers and seas—
Who has fathomed the heart!
Everything is in it—
Ships and storms, oars and boatmen.
There, in the heart, is the whole wide world,
Vast like a tent outstretched.
He who learns the secret of the heart
Comes to know God.

Sultan Bahu

When my heart is free, unburdened, open to receiving love, I experience God. When I express this love energy in the world, I become a sacred artist translating God's energy into expression.

Richard Hatch

Being mortal, never pray for an untroubled life. Rather, ask the gods to give you an enduring heart.

Menander

The purpose of life is to increase the warm heart.

the Dalai Lama

Forget not the central truth, that God is seated in your own heart.

Swami Ramdas

It is a burning of the heart that I want; it is this burning that is everything, more precious than the empire of the world, because it calls God secretly in the night.

Rumi

If you want to love, take the time to listen to your heart. In most ancient and wise cultures it is a regular practice for people to talk to their heart. There are rituals, stories, and meditative skills in every spiritual tradition that awaken the voice of the heart. To live wisely, this practice is essential, because our heart is the source of our connection to and intimacy with all of life.

Jack Kornfield

Listen to your heart. It knows all things, because it came from the soul of the world, and it will one day return there.

Paulo Coelho

 Intuition

In this culture, we speak of making decisions as "making up our minds." We trust the rational process, and when we ask each other for reasons, we want to know "What were you thinking?" All of this presupposes that we have a mind that can think clearly without the contaminations of the passions, the emotions, the visions and desires and influences that we may not even be aware of. All of this presupposes that the mind and the thoughts are the most logical place from which to make decisions.

But what if they're not? What if, instead of going up into our heads, we go down and "make up our hearts" or "make up our souls" instead? What if we ask each other "What were you feeling?" What if "I just felt it was right for me" was enough reason, enough explanation and rationalization and analysis, enough of a logical answer to convince us that the decision was right?

I like what Eileen Caddy advises. "Cease trying to work everything out with your minds. It will get you nowhere. Live by intuition and inspiration and let your whole life be Revelation." I disagree with her absolutism here—

sometimes our minds *do* get us somewhere, and somewhere important—but on the whole, we would find ourselves much more connected to our spirituality, much more open to revelation, if we put feelings in our thoughts and lived by our intuition.

By learning to contact, listen to, and act on our intuition, we can directly connect to a higher power of the universe and allow it to become our guiding force.

Shakti Gawain

It is always with excitement that I wake up in the morning wondering what my intuition will toss up to me, like gifts from the sea. I work with it and rely on it. It's my partner.

Dr. Jonas Salk

Intuition is the deepest wisdom of the soul.

Jeffrey Mishlove

Most of us are living at the periphery of consciousness while intuition invites us into the center.

Willis Harman

Human beings have an intuitive capacity and knowledge (what the romantic poets called *sensibility*) that somewhere at the center of life is something ineffably and unalterably right and good, and that this "rightness" can be discovered through artistic and spiritual explorations that have been honored by all the great perennial religious traditions.

David Whyte

The intuitive mind is a sacred gift and the rational mind is a faithful servant. We have created a society that honors the servant and has forgotten the gift.

Albert Einstein

[Intuition is] the inner knowing that helps us arrive at the right place at the right time so that we can be swept away by the benevolent flow of synchronicity that gets us where we're meant to be as easily as the Universe can arrange it.

Sarah Ban Breathnach

. . . Intuition is really a sudden immersion of the soul into the universal current of life, where the histories of all people are connected, and we are able to know everything, because it's all written there.

Paulo Coelho

For the spiritual being, intuition is far more than a hunch. It is viewed as guidance or as God talking, and this inner insight is never taken lightly or ignored.

Wayne Dyer

Intuitive knowledge is an illumination of the soul, whereby it beholds in the light of God those things which it pleases Him to reveal to us by a direct impression of divine clearness.

René Descartes

Some of my best insights have come to me through what I can only call a mystical process. It's like having God whisper in your ear.

Candace Pert

Whereas we can reach the intellect only through thinking, we can reach the spirit only through intuition. The practice of meditation is simply the deepening, broadening, and strengthening of intuition. A mystical experience is simply a prolonged intuition.

Paul Brunton

Letting Go

In the world's wisdom traditions, there is much written about the importance of letting go, which is at various times and with varying nuances known as detachment, nonattachment, surrender, renunciation, submitting to the will of God, or "letting go and letting God." The Buddha taught, "In the end these things matter most: How well did you love? How fully did you love? How deeply did you learn to let go?" Poetry is also full of such lessons in letting go. In Mary Oliver's brilliant poem "In Blackwater Woods," she ends by saying

> To live in this world
>
> you must be able
> to do three things:
> to love what is mortal;
> to hold it
>
> against your bones knowing
> your own life depends on it;
> and, when the time comes to let it go,
> to let it go.

Letting go of what and whom we love can be difficult, painful, gut-clenching, and heart-wrenching, but in letting go of what is material and mortal, we learn lessons in what is spiritual and immortal. By letting go of having things turn out *our* way, and surrendering to divine will, we allow things to turn out the *divine* way, or what Taoists simply call The Way.

The depth of one's letting go determines the depth of one's freedom.

Karen Goldman

"Let go and let God." Effort will take you only so far. There's always a gap when you're trying to reach infinity. You can count forever and not reach infinity. The maximum experience the mind can have is the concept of God, but not the experience of God. There is always a gap. To cross that gap, you need to be able to surrender.

Gurucharan Singh Khalsa

Drop the last year into the silent limbo of the past.
Let it go, for it was imperfect, and thank God that it can go.

Brooks Atkinson

Renunciation: making yourself more available, more gentle and open to others. The warrior who has accomplished true renunciation is completely naked and raw. He has no desire to manipulate situations. He is able to be, quite fearlessly, what he is. The result of this letting go is that he discovers a bank of self-existing energy that is always available. It is the energy of basic goodness.

Chogyam Trungpa

For this is Wisdom; to love, to live
To take what fate, or the Gods may give.
To ask no question, to make no prayer,
To kiss the lips and caress the hair,
Speed passion's ebb as you greet its flow
To have,—to hold—and—in time,—let go!

Laurence Hope

Do everything with a mind that lets go. Don't accept praise or gain or anything else. If you let go a little you will have a little peace; if you let go a lot you will have a lot of peace; if you let go completely you will have complete peace.

Ajahn Chah

To me, getting in touch with the experience of God is a question of letting go. It's what the Indian teachings talk about as nonattachment. They talk about letting go of our desires, letting go of our beliefs and preconceptions. When that happens, we naturally experience ourselves as we are—without the self-talk in our heads that keeps us from our experience of God. For me, relaxation is the essence of letting go—relaxation of the body, mind, heart, and soul; relaxing all the different parts of our being. Meditation is the art of relaxing all our different dimensions. Besides relaxing the body, meditation relaxes the mind from all its caught-upness in worldly thoughts; it relaxes the heart so we can experience forgiveness and compassion. When we learn to relax our attention, we begin to experience the inner world more clearly.

Peter Russell

 Living

If I had to shrink this book down from 110 to just one way of connecting with our spiritual nature, the one I would choose is living. It seems simplistic, but often the simplest truth is rich with wisdom.

But like everything else, living becomes a spiritual experience only when we see it as one. We must attend to our lives; we must cherish living. Elisabeth Kübler-Ross says, "Our concern must be to live while we're alive."

A simple truth, yes, but one easy to embody? No. The words of Frederick Buechner can guide us.

Listen to your life. See it for the fathomless mystery that it is.
In the boredom and pain of it no less than in the excitement and gladness:
touch, taste, smell your way to the holy and hidden heart of it
because in the last analysis all moments are key moments,
and life itself is grace.

Just to be is a blessing. Just to live is holy.

Rabbi Abraham Heschel

Everything is extraordinarily clear. I see the whole landscape before
me, I see my hands, my feet, my toes, and I smell the rich river mud.
I feel a sense of tremendous strangeness and wonder at being alive.
Wonder of wonders.

Buddha

Once out of all the gray days of my life I have looked into the heart
of reality; I have witnessed the truth; I have seen life as it really is—
ravishingly, ecstatically, madly beautiful, and filled to overflowing
with a wild joy, and a value unspeakable.

Margaret Prescott Montague

Until you know that life is interesting—and find it so—
you haven't found your soul.

Geoffrey Fisher

While we have the gift of life, it seems to me the only tragedy is to
allow part of us to die whether it is our spirit, our creativity, or
our glorious uniqueness.

Gilda Radner

Your life is the one place you have to spend yourself fully—wild, generous, *drastic*—in an unrationed profligacy of self. . . . And in that split second when you understand you finally are about to die—to uncreate the world no time to do it over no more chances—that instant when you realize your conscious existence is truly flaring nova, won't you want to have used up all—*all*—the splendor that you are?

Robin Morgan

I like living. I have sometimes been wildly despairing, acutely miserable, racked with sorrow, but through it all I still know quite certainly that just to *be* alive is a grand thing.

Agatha Christie

For everything that lives is holy
Life delights in life.

William Blake

One thing I know. If living isn't a seeking for the grail
it may be a damned amusing game.

F. Scott Fitzgerald

I think what we're seeking is an experience of being alive, so that our life experiences on the purely physical plane will have resonance within our own innermost being and reality, so that we actually feel the rapture of being alive.

Joseph Campbell

Losing Ourselves

It may sound like a play on words or a paradox when I assert that when we find ourselves, we find ourselves to be divine, but also when we lose ourselves, we find ourselves to be divine. However, this makes complete sense if we imagine that the self we must lose is the ego-self, making room for the influx of the divine-self; as Robert Musil writes, "The end of man is to let the spirit in him permeate his whole being, his soul, flesh, and affections. He attains his deepest self by losing his selfish ego."

Take to heart Mahmud Shabistari's advice: "Go sweep the chamber of your heart. Make it ready to be the dwelling place of the Beloved. When you depart, He will enter it. In you, empty of yourself, He will display all his beauty." Clearing out our ego, we make a space and welcome Spirit to dwell within.

As the soul becomes more pure and bare and poor, and possesses less of created things, and is emptied of all things that are not God, it receives God more purely, and is more completely in Him; and it truly becomes one with God, and it looks into God and God into it, face to face as it were; two images transformed into one. Some simple folk think that they will see God as if He were standing there and they here. It is not so. God and I, we are one.

Meister Eckhart

Yield and overcome;
Bend and be straight;
Empty and be full.

the Tao Te Ching

I need nothing but God, and to lose myself in the heart of God.

Saint Margaret Mary Alacoque

As human beings we are made to surpass ourselves and are
truly ourselves only when transcending ourselves.

Huston Smith

Before there can be fullness there must be emptiness. Before God
can fill us with Himself we must first be emptied of ourselves.

A. W. Tozer

Slowly I begin the final metamorphosis. I must drive out my
old self and let the universe in.

David Malouf

The true value of a human being can be found in the degree
to which he has attained liberation from the self.

Albert Einstein

There is no room for God in him who is full of himself.

Hasidic proverb

Experiencing God gives me a sense of tremendous peacefulness and
love—of losing my boundaries. I feel connected with something much
larger than myself. I feel very much alive, as if I can feel the life force
in every cell of my body.

Joan Borysenko

Develop an interest in life as you see it; the people, things, literature,
music—the world is so rich, simply throbbing with rich treasures,
beautiful souls, and interesting people. Forget yourself.

Henry Miller

Your duty is to be, and not to be this or that. "I am that I am" sums up the whole truth: the method is summarised in "Be still." And what does this stillness mean? It means "destroy yourself," because every name and form is the cause of trouble.

Ramana Maharshi

To know yourself or study yourself is to forget yourself, and if you forget yourself then you become enlightened by all things.

Dogen

It's only by forgetting yourself that you draw near to God.

Henry David Thoreau

Marriage

I get so frustrated when I hear people ranting about how gays want to desecrate the sacred bond of marriage by having their relationships recognized as such. "Don't you understand," I want to yell at the radio or newspaper or television or person in front of me, "that it's precisely because gays *know* that marriage is sacred that they want to partake in the practice?" If anyone's making a mockery of marriage, it's the gay people who *don't* want to marry, who criticize marriage for being profane and dysfunctional and want nothing to do with it. And the reason they want nothing to do with it is that *straight* people have made a mockery of marriage by desecrating their sacred vows.

Marriage between any two people *is* sacred, though as Cecil Myers says, an even better marriage is a threesome: "Successful marriage is always a triangle: a man, a woman, and God." Marriage, or any relationship, is always more successful, more beautiful, more sacred, and more alive when the holy spirit is an active presence, when the divine nature of the couple and their union is recognized and encouraged.

Marriages are made in heaven
and consummated on Earth.

John Lyly

When people get married because they think it's a long-time love affair,
they'll be divorced very soon, because all love affairs end in disappoint-
ment. But marriage is a recognition of a spiritual identity.

Joseph Campbell

Marriage is an Athenic weaving together of families, of two souls with
their individual fates and destinies, of time and eternity—everyday life
married to the timeless mysteries of the soul.

Thomas Moore

Heaven will be no heaven to me if I do not meet my wife there.

Andrew Jackson

The marriage state, with and without the affection suitable to it,
is the completest image of Heaven and Hell we are capable of
receiving in this life.

Sir Richard Steele

Two souls with but a single thought,
Two hearts that beat as one.

Friedrich Halm

I have found the one whom my soul loves.

Song of Solomon 3:4

Marriage is a coming together for better or for worse, hopefully enduring, and intimate to the degree of being sacred.

William O. Douglas

A successful marriage requires falling in love many times, always with the same person.

Germaine Greer

Marriage is an act of will that signifies and involves a mutual gift, which unites the spouses and binds them to their eventual souls, with whom they make up a sole family—a domestic church.

John Paul II

A happy marriage perhaps represents the ideal of human relationship— a setting in which each partner, while acknowledging the need of the other, feels free to be what he or she by nature is: a relationship in which instinct as well as intellect can find expression; in which giving and taking are equal; in which each accepts the other, and I confront Thou.

Anthony Storr

Love at first sight is easy to understand; it's when two people have been looking at each other for a lifetime that it becomes a miracle.

Sam Levenson

For two people in a marriage to live together day after day is unquestionably the one miracle the Vatican has overlooked.

Bill Cosby

Marriage [is] not just a bond between two people but a bond between those two people and . . . their children, and their neighbors . . . lovers must not . . . live for themselves alone. They must turn from their gaze at one another back toward the community. . . . The marriage of two lovers joins them to one another, to forebears, to descendants, to the community, to Heaven and earth. It is the fundamental connection without which nothing holds, and trust is its necessity.

Wendell Berry

 ## Miracles

Everything is a miracle. What further miracles do you want?
Look below you: even the humblest blade of grass
has its guardian angel who stands by and helps it to grow.
Look about you: what a miracle is the star-filled sky!
And if you close your eyes: what a miracle the world within us!
What a star-filled sky is our heart!

Nikos Kazantzakis

Einstein counsels us, "There are only two ways to live your life. One is as though nothing is a miracle. The other is as though everything is a miracle." Kazantzakis, Einstein, and other spiritual seekers have chosen the latter, to see everything as a miracle. That includes ourselves, for as Ray Bradbury says, "We are the miracle of force and matter making itself over into imagination and will. Incredible. The Life Force experimenting with forms. You for one. Me for another. The Universe has shouted itself alive. We are one of the shouts."

The purpose of miracles is to teach us to see the miraculous everywhere.

Saint Augustine of Hippo

I'm passionately involved in life: I love its color, its movement.
To be alive, to be able to see, to walk, to have houses, music, paintings—
it's all a miracle.

Arthur Rubinstein

The miracles of the church seem to me to rest not so much upon faces
or voices or healing power coming suddenly near to us from afar off,
but upon our perceptions being made finer, so that for a moment our
eyes can see and our ears can hear what is there about us always.

Willa Cather

For the truly faithful, no miracle is necessary. For those who doubt,
no miracle is sufficient.

Nancy Gibbs

I think miracles exist in part as gifts and in part as clues that there
is something beyond the flat world we see.

Peggy Noonan

Everything is a miracle. It is a miracle that one does not dissolve
in one's bath like a lump of sugar.

Pablo Picasso

The miracle on earth are the laws of heaven.

Jean Paul Richter

Every believer is God's miracle.

Philip James Bailey

Miracles occur naturally as expressions of love. The real miracle
is the love that inspires them. In this sense everything that comes
from love is a miracle.

Marianne Williamson

The invariable mark of wisdom is to see the miraculous in the common.

Ralph Waldo Emerson

The age of miracles is forever here.

Thomas Carlyle

Miracles are God's coups d'etat.

Anne-Sophie Swetchine

There is a dance of miracles
holding hands in a chain around the earth
and out through space to the moon,
and to the stars and beyond the stars;
And to behold this dance is enough:
So much brighter, and secret looking,
and glimpses of wonder and dreams of terror.
It is enough! It is enough!

James Oppenheim

 Mystery

I once went to a funeral service where a lay preacher listed the four greatest
mysteries everyone must grapple with: Where did we come from? How
shall we live our lives? What is the purpose of our lives? What happens

when we die? The preacher, a young man still in his twenties, said, "I am here to tell you the answers," which he then proceeded to do as matter-of-factly as if he were a waiter telling us the specials of the day.

I was amazed by his confidence, the assurance with which he imparted the answers to the questions that people have pondered for time eternal. At first I found it sweet—and later, a little scary, too—that his religion offered him and his congregation the quick comfort of answers and protected him, and them, from the unfathomable depths of the questions. I was reminded of Albert Einstein's speculation that "it was the experience of mystery—even if mixed with fear—that engendered religion." Further, I wondered if one of the distinctions between being religious and being spiritual has to do with an attitude toward mystery—that religions try to explain and contain the mysteries of life, but that spirituality embraces mysteries, even courts them, favoring the process of questioning over the product of answering.

Regardless of the answer to that line of questioning, I returned to Einstein, with whom I agree that "the most beautiful thing we can experience is the mysterious. It is the source of all true art and science. He to whom this emotion is a stranger, who can no longer pause to wonder and stand rapt in awe, is as good as dead: his eyes are closed."

Let us not forget that even for the most contemporary thinker, who sees a majesty and grandeur in natural law, science cannot explain everything. We all still have to face the ultimate miracle—the origin and principle of life. This is the supreme mystery that is the essence of worship and without which there can be no religion. In the presence of this mystery all peoples must take an attitude much like that of an Indian, who beholds with awe the Divine in all creation.

Ohiyesa

God moves in a mysterious way
His wonders to perform.

William Cowper

What the word *God* means is the mystery really. It's the mystery that we face as humans. The mystery of existence, of suffering, and of death. The question is: What is your relationship to the mystery? Are you defending yourself from it? Are you making love to it? Are you living in it?

Ram Dass

Respect for mystery, sense of the mystery of God, veneration of the sacredness of mystery, awe and humility in approaching the ineffable holiness of Him who can be known in Himself only by His own revelation of Himself—these are essential virtues of a truly religious soul.

Thomas Merton

Give exceeding thanks for the mystery which remains a mystery still—the veil that hides you from the infinite, which makes it possible for you to believe in what you cannot see.

Robert Nathan

Religion points to that area of human experience where in one way or another man comes upon mystery as a summons to pilgrimage.

Frederick Buechner

The workings of the human heart are the profoundest mystery of the universe. One moment they make us despair of our kind, and the next we see in them the reflection of the divine image.

Charles W. Chesnutt

It began in mystery, and it will end in mystery, but what a savage and beautiful country lies in between.

Diane Ackerman

Mystery has its own mysteries, and there are gods above gods.
We have ours, they have theirs. That is what's known as infinity.

Jean Cocteau

 Pregnancy and Birth

I have never been pregnant or given birth, and like many others in my position, I look upon those who have with an odd mix of awe and envy. I can't help feeling like they know something specific that I don't know, that they've experienced something that can't be experienced in any other way, something at once physical and spiritual, at once magical and mundane. Perhaps pregnancy and birth are the most elevated way to experience the intersection between the sacred and the profane: the discomfort and pain in both bodies, one feeling like it's dying as one struggles to be born, one body stretched to its outer limit to give birth to the limitless spirit inside of a brand-new body. It is the replaying of an ancient story; the sacrifice of the body on a cross of pain to bring forth new life, the combination of suffering and joy, of agony and ecstasy, of body and spirit that marks the experience of being alive in this world.

Simply said, "Birthing is the most profound initiation a woman can have" (Robin Lim).

At a birth the heavens lean down, or perhaps it is that the racked body
is spun fine to be aware of eternal things. We women hardly know
how lucky we are in this.

Katherine Trevelyan

Every person is a God in embryo. Its only desire is to be born.

Deepak Chopra

The first thing which I can record concerning myself is, that I was born. These are wonderful words. This life, to which neither time nor eternity can bring diminution—this everlasting living soul, began. My mind loses itself in these depths.

Margaret Oliphant

Birth is the sudden opening of a window, through which you look out upon a stupendous prospect. For what has happened? A miracle. You have exchanged nothing for the possibility of everything.

William MacNeile Dixon

Our birth is but a sleeping and a forgetting;
The soul that rises with us, our life's Star,
Hath had elsewhere its setting,
And cometh from afar; Not in entire forgetfulness,
And not in utter nakedness,
But trailing clouds of glory do we come
From God who is our home.

William Wordsworth

Nothing is more magical than the birth of a child, except perhaps watching that infant grow into a person as the soul emerges gradually and shows itself in the individuality of a new being.

Thomas Moore

Pregnancy offers you an opportunity to experience a heightened sense of your spirituality . . . it is a period of time during which your connection with something beyond yourself is more apparent than in a nonpregnant state—it is at once physical and transcendental.

Aviva Jill Romm

There is power that comes to women when they give birth. They don't ask for it, it simply invades them. Accumulates like clouds on the horizon and passes through, carrying the child with it.

Sheryl Feldman

Happiness, joy, awe, wonder—to think of a baby, a new life growing within—what a miracle.

Lisa Oklo

Pregnancy is the only time in a woman's life she can help God work a miracle.

Erma Bombeck

Children are a heritage of the Lord; the fruit of the womb is his reward.

Psalms 127:3

Pregnant women! They had that weird frisson, an aura of magic that combined awkwardly with an earthy sense of duty. Mundane, because they were nothing unique on the suburban streets; ethereal because their attention was ever somewhere else. Whatever you said was trivial. And they had that preciousness which they imposed wherever they went, compelling attention, constantly reminding you that they carried the future inside, its contours already drawn, but veiled, private, an inner secret.

Ruth Morgan

As often as I have witnessed the miracle, held the perfect creature with its tiny hands and feet, each time I have felt as though I were entering a cathedral with prayer in my heart.

Margaret Sanger

The shamans are forever yacking about their snake oil miracles.
I prefer the real McCoy, a pregnant woman.

Robert Heinlein

Recognizing the Divine in Everything

There is a Gnostic idea that God did not create the world, but that He emanated or brought forth from himself the substance of all that is in the world. Since everything emanated from a divine source, everything has divinity as its source, which some more colorfully refer to as divine sparks or "God-sparks."

If we could wish for one ability that would allow us to remain in constant connection with our spiritual natures, it might be for the wisdom to recognize the God-sparks everywhere, an ability that Marie de L'Incarnation refers to as

Seeing God in everything
and everything in God
with completely extraordinary clearness
and delicacy.

and what Brother Lawrence refers to as

The pure, loving gaze
that finds God
everywhere.

See God in every person, place, and thing,
and all will be well in your world.

Louise Hay

The highest condition of the religious sentiment is when . . .
the worshiper not only sees God everywhere, but sees nothing
which is not full of God.

Harriet Martineau

If someone were to ask me whether I believed in God, or saw God, or had
a particular relationship with God, I would reply that I don't separate
God from my world in my thinking. I feel that God is everywhere.
That's why I never feel separated from God or feel I must seek God,
any more than a fish in the ocean feels it must seek water. In a sense,
God is the "ocean" in which we live.

Robert Fulghum

I encounter God as a seductive sense of something just behind the veils
of form. Hanuman, who is part of the Hindu pantheon, says, "When
I don't know who I am, I serve God. When I do know who I am, I am
God." That describes the funny in-and-out quality of my experience of
God. When I'm feeling separate, I see God in everything around me. I
look at people, and I see them as God in disguise. But when I am quiet
in meditation and I experience gratitude for the grace of it all, I allow my
unworthiness to go, so that I can start to feel as if God and I are one.

Ram Dass

We should understand well that all things are the work of the Great
Spirit. We should know the Great Spirit is within all things: the trees,
the grasses, the rivers, the mountains, and the four-legged and winged
peoples: and even more important, we should understand that the
Great Spirit is also above all these things and peoples. When we
understand all this deeply in our hearts, then we will fear, and love,
and know the Great Spirit, and then we will be and act and live
as the Great Spirit intends.

Black Elk

Apprehend God in all things, for God is in all things. Every single creature is full of God, and is a book about God. If I spend enough time with the tiniest creature—even a caterpillar—I would never have to prepare a sermon. So full of God is every creature.

Meister Eckhart

What excitement will renew your body
When we all begin to see
That His Heart resides in
Everything?

God has a root in each act and creature
That He draws His mysterious
Divine life from!

Hafiz

In the faces of men and women I see God,
and in my own face in the glass,
I find letters from God dropt in the street,
and everyone is sign'd by God's name.
And I leave them where they are,
for I know that wheresoe'er I go,
Others will punctually come for ever and ever.

Walt Whitman

 The Spirit Within

Where there are humans
You'll find flies,
And Buddhas.

Kobayashi Issa's simple haiku points to a spiritual truth, that anywhere there are humans, there are gods within—still human, as the flies attest to, but Buddhas, nonetheless. "Really great men," says John Ruskin, "see something divine in every other man." It's not an easy task sometimes, partly because, let's face it, some people hide their divinity pretty deep inside, but partly because we are simply not trained to see each other or relate to each other that way. In fact, says Stan Dale, "If God wanted to hide, He would hide in human beings because that's the last place we would think to look."

For some of us, the harder task is not to find the Buddha in another, but to find it within. Though we extol the virtue of self-esteem, we stop far short of suggesting we esteem the god within. Some would even consider that blasphemous. However, if we really want to connect with our spirits, we must do what a character in Ntosake Shange's play *for colored girls who have considered suicide/when the rainbow is enuf* does:

I found god in myself
& i loved her / i loved her fiercely

Each one of us reflects the mystery of the universe. Each of us has a
consciousness that partakes in the soul of the universe. When we
understand this and see the same power in everyone, we learn to truth
ourselves and others. That trust is the love we share with humanity. . . .
I say that once you find clarity of soul, you will trust every other soul.

Rudolfo Anaya

Consider for once, that there is nothing in heaven or in earth that is not also in man. In him is God who is also in Heaven; and all the forces of Heaven operate likewise in man. Where else can Heaven be rediscovered if not in man?

Paracelsus

The religion of the twenty-first century is the recognition that in our frail and weary human form there is something incredibly divine. It has been there all along, but we were dreaming, with eyes that looked outward, instead of awakening, with inner vision.

Christopher H. Jackson

God became man so that man may become God.

Saint Athanasius

I believe that God is in me, as the sun is in the color and fragrance of the flower, the Light in my darkness, the Voice in my silence.

Helen Keller

Know thyself, O divine lineage in mortal guise!

Marsilio Ficino

Like every other being, I am a splinter of the infinite deity.

Carl Jung

For life means not only to live, but to ennoble oneself and reach that perfection which is the innate yearning of the soul. The solution to the problem of the day is the awakening of the consciousness of humanity to the divinity of man.

Hazrat Inayat Khan

The tragedy of the human race was that we had forgotten
we were each Divine.

Shirley Maclaine

For behold, the kingdom of God is within you.

Luke 17:21

The closest we can come to the experience of the Great Mystery is to
see God in one another. Remember that beyond all appearances of
separation, we are one with the Heart of Love.

Joan Borysenko

 ## Stillness

I like the word *still. Still* is different from *silent,* for one can be still and yet
be conversing. While it is similar to *inner peace,* I prefer *stillness,* prefer the
way when I draw out the beginning consonants in *sssssssttttill,* it sounds like
sssssshhhh. Stillness is a hush, the quieting of the chattering monkey mind
to make a space for the butterfly spirit to alight. Stillness is deep, but not
as deep as sleep, for we are wildly awake when we are still, awake only to
the presence of the divine that surrounds our being. "Be still," the psalm
advises, "and know that I am God." Simpler yet, be still, and know God.

Still your mind in me, still yourself in me,
And without doubt you shall be united with me,
Lord of Love, dwelling in your heart.

the Bhagavad Gita

In limpid souls God beholds his own image. He rests in them and they in Him. Nothing in all creation is so like God as stillness.

Meister Eckhart

For me, the experience of God means the experience of a very deep peace. I think we all crave mental stillness at this point. We need to drop the chatter, even transformational chatter. Sometimes, people ask me how to know what God is saying to them, as though His voice would have a certain tenor or something. But the voice of God is a small, still voice. We can only hear it when the mind is quiet.

Marianne Williamson

It is essential to know that to be a happy person, a happy family, a happy society, it is very crucial to have a good heart, that is very crucial. World peace must develop from inner peace. Peace is not just the absence of violence but the manifestation of human compassion.

the Dalai Lama

Just remaining quietly in the presence of God, listening to Him, being attentive to Him, requires a lot of courage and know-how.

Thomas Merton

Empty yourself of everything.
Let the mind rest at peace.
The ten thousand things rise and fall while the Self watches their return.
They grow and flourish and then return to the source.
Returning to the source is stillness, which is the way of nature.

the Tao Te Ching

Once the heart has been perfectly emptied of mental images, it gives birth to divine and mystical concepts that play within it, just as fish and dolphins play in a calm sea.

Hesychios

Stillness of spirit is an endless worship of God
And a standing in the very Presence.

Saint John Klimakos

Lord, my mind is not noisy with desires,
and my heart has satisfied its longing,
I do not care about religion
or anything that is not you.
I have soothed and quieted my soul,
like a child at its mother's breast.
My soul is as peaceful as a child
sleeping in its mother's arms.

Psalms 131

Men cannot see their reflection in running water, but only in still water. Only that which is itself still can still the seekers of stillness.

Chuang Tzu

To the mind that is still, the whole universe surrenders.

Lao Tzu

 Unity Consciousness

I believe in the absolute oneness of God and therefore also of
humanity. Though we have many bodies, we have but one soul.

Gandhi

One of the characteristics of mysticism is a recognition of unity, of the
oneness of humanity and God that Gandhi speaks of, multiple bodies but
"one soul." Many of us have had mystical moments where we recognize
and melt into this truth, but they are difficult to sustain in this world of
multiplicity.

Albert Einstein was a modern mystic who attained unity consciousness.
He shared his wisdom with us. "A human being is part of a whole, called
by us the Universe, a part limited in time and space. He experiences himself, his thoughts and feelings, as something separated from the rest—a
kind of optical delusion of his consciousness. This delusion is a kind of
prison for us, restricting us to our personal desires and to affection for a
few persons nearest us. Our task must be to free ourselves from this prison
by widening our circles of compassion to embrace all living creatures and
the whole of nature in its beauty."

Freeing ourselves from the delusion of separateness, we will learn to
see our bodies as one limb in the universal body, and our souls as one
facet of the universal soul.

I feel an indescribable ecstasy and delirium in melting, as it were, into
the system of beings, in identifying myself with the whole of nature.

John Rousseau

We are like waves that do not move individually but rise and fall in
rhythm. To share, to rise and fall in rhythm with life around us, is a
spiritual necessity.

Albert Schweitzer

The true sense of community lies in understanding our interconnectedness and acting from a sense of relatedness. It is a challenge. Let's begin at the beginning. That is where we can start to reweave the sacred web of life so that it once again becomes whole.

Suzanne Arms

Every heart is the other heart.
Every soul is the other soul.
Every face is the other face.
The individual is the one illusion.

Marguerite Young

To know others you do not have to go and knock on four billion separate doors. Once you have seen your real Self, you have seen the Self in all.

Eknath Easwaran

No individual exists in its own nature, independent of all other factors of life. Each has the totality of the Universe at its base. All individuals have, therefore, the whole Universe as their common ground, and this universality becomes conscious in the experience of enlightenment, in which the individual awakens into his own true all-embracing nature.

Lama Govinda

The first peace, which is the most important, is that which comes within the souls of people when they realize their relationship, their oneness with the universe and all its powers, and when they realize that at the center of the universe dwells the Great Spirit, and that this center is really everywhere, it is within each of us.

Black Elk

According to the true Indian view, our consciousness of the world, merely as the sum total of things that exist, and as governed by laws, is imperfect. But it is perfect when our consciousness realizes all things as spiritually one with it, and therefore capable of giving us joy. For us the highest purpose of this world is not merely living in it, knowing it and making use of it, but realizing our own selves in it through expansion of sympathy; not alienating ourselves from it and dominating it, but comprehending and uniting it with ourselves in perfect union.

Rabindranath Tagore

Everything in the universe is related; we are all connected; from stardust to human flesh, we vibrate with the same elements of the universe. The web of life is infused by spirit, and each one of us has the power to use that creative energy to manifest our potential.

Rudolfo Anaya

But one day when I was sitting quiet . . . it came to me that feeling of being part of everything, not separate at all. I knew that if I cut a tree, my arm would bleed.

Alice Walker

Recently when I found out that I had cancer, I had to come to grips with something I'd left out of my life for a long time. That's when I got in the habit of going out early in the morning before daylight and looking up into the heavens and becoming part of that. I said, "My God, I'm part of that; I'm part of eternity. This is me." And then I realized it makes no difference when you pass on to Glory, or when you die, if you feel that you are a part of this, all of this. Whatever we have achieved as far as intellect and spiritual growth are concerned, we still can't conceive of infinity. This is all part of me and I am part of every human life on this globe.

John Henry Faulk

THE NATURAL WORLD

The soul desires us and craves union with us. . . .
We don't necessarily get more soul in our lives
by doing things in a direct way than by allowing
ourselves to be distracted and enticed by the world's
beauty and interest. The world is alive and has a
body with private parts that can be alluring.

Thomas Moore

A soul who is not close to nature is far away from what
is called spirituality. In order to be spiritual one must
communicate, and especially one must communicate
with nature; one must feel nature.

Hazrat Inayat Khan

Animals

I have written most of this book with Samson, the smaller of my two Yorkshire terriers, on my lap. I did not invite him here; he insisted. In the beginning I saw him as needy, but then I began to see that in fact, it was *me* who was needy. When the words wouldn't flow, I took my hands off the keyboard and ran them along the length of his little body until they flowed again. When the ideas were blocked, I looked away from the computer screen and down at his open brown eyes until they became unblocked. Sometimes I would simply rest my hand on his chest and feel the miracle of his dog-lungs breathing, feel the beauty of his dog-heart beating. From source of nuisance to source of inspiration, Samson acted as a conduit of spirit, connecting me when I felt most disconnected.

Do you see what I mean about the needy one?

Anatole France wrote, "Until one has loved an animal, a part of one's soul remains unawakened." Those of us who love animals know this, know that there is a part of our hearts and souls reserved for and given solely to those creatures, that there is a part of our spirits that cannot be touched in any other way.

Can we open our hearts to the animals? Can we greet them as our soul mates, beings like ourselves who possess dignity and depth? To do so, we must learn to revere and respect the creatures who, like us, are a part of God's beloved creation, and to cherish the amazing planet that sustains our mutual existence. We must join in a biospirituality that will acknowledge and celebrate the sacred in all life.

Gary Kowalski

If thy heart were right, then every creature would be a mirror of life and a book of holy doctrine. There is no creature so small and abject, but it reflects the goodness of God.

Thomas à Kempis

Being with pets can often be a very prayerful activity as well. Animals are the highest form of aliveness that are still spontaneously transparent to the Divine. Humans have to work at that. Meeting an animal can be quite similar to meeting a very saintly person. They are totally transparent. When I look at a cat, it's like looking into God's eyes.

David Steindl-Rast

I love cats because I love my home and after a while they become its visible soul.

Jean Cocteau

Folks will know how large your soul is by the way you treat a dog.

Charles F. Duran

We can judge the heart of man by his treatment of animals.

Immanuel Kant

I care not much for a man's religion whose dog and cat are not the better for it.

Abraham Lincoln

You think that these dogs will not be in Heaven! I tell you they will be there long before any of us.

Robert Louis Stevenson

If I spent enough time with the tiniest creature—even a caterpillar— I would never have to prepare a sermon. So full of God is every creature.

Meister Eckhart

An animal's eyes have the power to speak a great language.

Martin Buber

If dogs are not there, it is not heaven.

Elisabeth M. Thomas

I hope you love birds too. It is economical. It saves going to heaven.

Emily Dickinson

 # Day

Yet, behind the night,
Waits for the great unborn, somewhere afar,
Some white tremendous daybreak.

Rupert Brooke

Dawn. Day breaks upon the horizon. The miracle of another sunrise; the miracle of another awakening. Don't get out of bed too soon. Lie there and witness the miracle of Light. Lie there and witness the miracle of Breath. Lie there and witness the miracle of Time.

Morning. We rise into the great unborn. We are still we, but what new me might we meet today? Coffee, tea, we break the fast of the night and fuel our bodies for the day.

Day. We enter the stage, the play, we give to our receptive world our gifts and receive from our giving world its gifts. We sustain and are sustained by the light of the day.

Dusk. Behind it, Night. Behind Night, Dawn. Lie there and witness the miracle of Time, of Breath, of Light.

Begin again with Day.

Today a new sun rises for me; everything lives, everything is animated, everything seems to speak to me of my passion, everything invites me to cherish it.

Anne de Lenclos

Whether one is twenty, forty, or sixty; whether one has succeeded, failed or just muddled along; whether yesterday was full of sun or storm, or one of those dull days with no weather at all, life begins each morning! . . . Each morning is the open door to a new world—new vistas, new aims, new tryings.

Leigh Mitchell Hodges

To be seeing the world made new every morning, as if it were the morning of the first day, and then to make the most of it for the individual soul as if each were the last day, is the daily curriculum of the mind's desire.

John H. Finley

Greet each day with your eyes open to beauty, your mind open to change, and your heart open to love.

Paula Finn

Do not say, "It is morning," and dismiss it with a name of yesterday. See it for the first time as a newborn child that has no name.

Rabindranath Tagore

There will be something, anguish or elation, that is peculiar to this day alone. I rise from sleep and say: Hail to the morning! Come down to me, my beautiful unknown.

Jessica Powers

The stillness of the early morning scene enables me to take in and enjoy many things which pass me by during the bustle of the day. First, there are the scents, which seem even more generous with their offerings than they are in the evening.

Rosemary Verey

We should live each day with a gentleness, a vigor, and a keenness of appreciation which are often lost when time stretches before us in the constant panorama of more days and months and years to come.

Helen Keller

Waking up in the morning, I vow with all beings
to be ready for sparks of the Dharma
from flowers or children or birds.

Robert Aitken

The moment when you first wake up in the morning is the most wonderful of the twenty-four hours. No matter how weary or dreary you may feel, you possess the certainty that, during the day that lies before you, absolutely anything may happen. And the fact that it practically always doesn't, matters not a jot. The possibility is always there.

Monica Baldwin

Each time dawn appears, the mystery is there in its entirety.

René Daumal

Wake at dawn with a winged heart and
give thanks for another day of loving.

Kahlil Gibran

 The Earth

George William Russell wrote about the many different ways our spirits can fall under the enchanting spell of the earth, and did so in words so powerful that this section needs no further introduction.

"So the lover of Earth obtains his reward, and little by little the veil is lifted of an inexhaustible beauty and majesty. It may be he will be tranced in some spiritual communion, or will find his being overflowing into the being of the elements, or become aware that they are breathing their life into his own. Or Earth may become on an instant, all faery to him, and earth and air resound with the music of its invisible people. Or the trees and rocks may waver before his eyes and become transparent, revealing what creatures were hidden from him by the curtain, and he will know as the ancients did of dryad and hamadryad, of genii of wood and mountain. Or Earth may suddenly blaze about him with supernatural light in some lonely spot amid the hills, and he will find he stands as the prophet in a place that is holy ground, and he may breathe the intoxicating exhalations as did the sibyls of old. Or his love may hurry him away in dream to share in deeper mysteries, and he may see the palace chambers of nature where the wise ones dwell in secret, looking out over the nations, breathing power into this man's heart or that man's brain, on any who appear to their vision to wear the colour of truth. So gradually the earth lover realizes the golden world is all about him in imperishable beauty, and he may pass from the vision to the profounder beauty of being, and know an eternal love is within and around him, pressing upon him and sustaining with infinite tenderness his body, his soul, and his spirit."

> My soul can find no staircase to Heaven
> unless it be through Earth's loveliness.
>
> Michelangelo Buonardo

I am not an atheist but an earthiest. Be true to the earth.

Edward Abbey

Earth's crammed with Heaven, and every common bush afire with God.

Elizabeth Barrett Browning

God owns heaven, but He craves the earth.

Anne Sexton

It is a wholesome and necessary thing for us to turn again to the earth and in the contemplation of her beauties to know the sense of wonder and humility.

Rachel Carson

The true miracle is not walking on water or walking in air, but simply walking on this earth.

Thich Nhat Hanh

Touch the earth, love the earth, honour the earth, her plains, her valleys, her hills, and her seas; rest your spirit in her solitary places.

Henry Beston

Our highest assurance of the goodness of providence rests in the flowers. All other things—our powers, our desires, our food—are necessary for our existence, but the rose is an extra. Its smell and its color are an embellishment of life, not a condition of it. It is only goodness which gives extras, and so we have much to hope from the flowers.

Sir Arthur Conan Doyle

Go out, go out I beg of you.
And taste the beauty of the wild.
Behold the miracle of the earth.
With all the wonder of a child.

Edna Jaques

Heaven is under our feet as well as over our heads.

Henry David Thoreau

Thus you can throw yourself flat on the ground, stretched out upon
Mother Earth, with the certain conviction that you are one with her
and she with you. You are as firmly established, as invulnerable as she,
indeed a thousand times firmer and more invulnerable. As surely as she
will engulf you tomorrow, so surely will she bring you forth anew to the
new striving and suffering. And not merely "some day." Now, today, every
day she is bringing you forth, not once but thousands upon thousands
of times, just as every day she engulfs you a thousand times over.

Erwin Schrödinger

 Flowers

In my bedroom hangs a Marc Chagall print in which an angel is hovering
over a bouquet of fresh flowers, her hand over her heart as if moved by
the beauty and the scent. "Art," Chagall wrote, "is the increasing effort
to compete with the beauty of flowers—and never succeeding," though in
this painting, he clearly succeeded with his beautiful flowers in seducing
the heart of an angel.

Juxtapose this image with another: One of the sweetest memories I have
of my now-deceased grandfather is of him going outside every day to cut
fresh roses and bring them in to my grandmother. I imagine he knew

what botanist Luther Burbank knew, that "flowers always make people better, happier, and more helpful; they are sunshine, food, and medicine to the soul," and what Mohammed knew and said in the Koran, that "bread feeds the body, indeed, but flowers feed also the soul." I imagine his trips out to the garden and back with those roses as one of his ways of feeding and nurturing the soul of my grandmother, seducing the heart of his angel.

Every morning I go outside now and cut fresh flowers, often roses, from my own garden. It is a tradition that I joyfully carry on, sometimes to feed and nurture my own soul, sometimes to seduce the heart of my beloved, sometimes to connect with the soul of my grandfather, and always, to invite the presence of the angels inside.

Paradise—
I see flowers
from the cottage where I lie.

Yaitsu

The flower is the poetry of reproduction.
It is an example of the eternal seductiveness of life.

Jean Giraudoux

A morning-glory at my window satisfies me more
than the metaphysics of books.

Walt Whitman

Flowers have spoken to me more than I can tell in written words. They are the hieroglyphics of angels, loved by all men for the beauty of the character, though few can decipher even fragments of their meaning.

Lydia M. Child

As I hold the flower in my hand and think of trying to describe it,
I realize how poor a creature I am,
how impotent are words in the presence of such perfection.

Celia Thaxter

Each flower is a soul blossoming in nature.

Gérard de Nerval

Flower in the crannied wall,
I pluck you out of the crannies,
I hold you, root and all, in my hand,
Little flower—but if I could understand
What you are, root and all and all in all,
I should know what God and man is.

Alfred, Lord Tennyson

The Amen of nature is always a flower.

Oliver Wendell Holmes

Arranging a bowl of flowers in the morning can give a sense of quiet
in a crowded day—like writing a poem, or saying a prayer.

Anne Morrow Lindbergh

Correct handling of flowers refines the personality.

Bokuyo Takeda

If we could see the miracle of a single flower clearly,
our whole life would change.

Buddha

 Mountains

The night before Martin Luther King, Jr., was assassinated, he gave a speech in support of striking sanitation workers in Memphis. His voice rose to a fevered pitch as he neared the end. "Well, I don't know what will happen now. We've got some difficult days ahead. But it doesn't matter with me now. Because I've been to the mountaintop. . . . And I've seen the promised land. I may not get there with you. But I want you to know tonight, that we, as a people, will get to the promised land. And I'm happy, tonight. I'm not worried about anything. I'm not fearing any man. Mine eyes have seen the glory of the coming of the Lord."

Heights have long been associated with spirituality. Even before most monotheistic religions associated the heavens with Heaven, most polytheistic religions had gods who lived in high places, most commonly on mountaintops. So when King's eyes had seen the glory of the coming of the Lord from the mountaintop, he situated himself in a long line of cultures and religions whose gods are associated with mountains: the Indian god Shiva's home is Mount Kailas in Tibet; the Japanese goddess Sengen's home is Mount Fuji in Japan; the Greek pantheon made their home on Mount Olympus; Mount Agung is the home of the Balinese gods; and T'ai Shan in China is a mountain that is considered to be a god itself. Many mountains are considered to be sacred, like Machu Picchu in Peru, where a temple was built to the gods, like Mount Sinai in Egypt, where Moses met with God and brought back the Ten Commandments, and like the Four Sacred Mountains that the Navajo believe the gods placed especially for them to live amongst.

We don't have to visit a sacred mountain to reap spiritual benefits; with our intention, we can make any mountain sacred. Nor do we have to physically ascend the mountain; with our attention, we can scale it with our eyes and feel its spiritual power. From the mountains, we can all be Kings who "can see the glory of the coming of the Lord."

Ascend a mountain, feel the freshness of the air, bathe in the chilly water of a mountain river, look at those enormous stones which are much older than you, and harmony will settle your soul.

Maria Barannikova

Nature is another important aspect of nourishing the soul. After a hike in the mountains where we live, for instance, I feel a remarkable sense of gratitude and awe. My mind quiets down and allows me to see more clearly the beauty of creation. And through that gratitude, the beauty of the universe is reflected back to the creator.

Joan Borysenko

Walk away quietly in any direction and taste the freedom of the mountaineer . . . climb the mountains and get their good tidings. Nature's peace will flow into you as sunshine flows into trees. The winds will blow their freshness into you, and the storms their energy, while cares will drop off like autumn leaves.

John Muir

Go out alone on the hills and listen. You will hear much: the winds will hold for you something more than sound; the voice of the stream will not be merely the babbling of hurrying waters. The trees and flowers are not so separate from you as they are at other times, but very near; the same substance, the same rhythm, the same song binds you to them. Alone amidst nature, a person learns to be one with all and all with One.

Frank Smythe

Mountains are giant, restful, absorbent. You can heave your spirit into a mountain and the mountain will keep it folded, and not throw it back as some creeks will.

Annie Dillard

We have all of us had our "moments" either on the mountains, or perhaps in some distant view of them, when life and joy have assumed new meanings and the world's horizon suddenly broken down and shown us realms of dream beyond and yet beyond.

Francis William Bourdillon

The color of the mountains is Buddha's body; the sound of running water is his great speech.

Zen Master Dogen

 # Nature

The first act of awe,
when man was struck
with the beauty or wonder of Nature,
was the first spiritual experience.

Henryk Skolimowski

Though Skolimowski is speculating about the first spiritual experience of primitive man, I would speculate that it remains true for us today: that if you polled the majority of us "modern" folks, we would recount an experience in or with nature as our first conscious spiritual experience as well. What makes nature such a carrier of spirituality is obvious, but what makes it such a popular carrier is the fact that there are as many different ways to experience spirituality in nature as there are different types of personalities. For example, some might find a spiritual connection while camping, others while driving to and through beautiful places; some might find it watching the Discovery Channel and marveling at Nature's mysteries and intricacies, while others might find it climbing to the peak of a mountain to photograph the beauty of the valley below; there are some who would find it sitting on a bench under a tree in their backyard, while others will find it holding on for dear life to a raft raging down the treacherous waters of a wild river. Like a good mother who favors none of her children and can nurture them all alike, Mother Nature has something to offer each of us—whether we feel more spiritually connected to butterflies or to dinosaurs, to deserts or to rain forests, to flora or to fauna—she can hold us in her enormous arms and offer us the world.

I love to think of nature as an unlimited broadcasting station through which God speaks to us every hour, if we will only tune in.

George Washington Carver

Every walk to the woods is a religious rite, every bath in the stream is a saving ordinance. Communion service is at all hours, and the bread and wine are from the heart and marrow of Mother Earth.

John Burroughs

Art is man's nature: Nature is God's art.

Philip James Bailey

Everybody needs beauty as well as bread, places to play in and pray in, where nature may heal and cheer and give strength to body and soul alike.

John Muir

The emotion felt by a person in the presence of nature certainly counts for something in the origin of religions.

Henry Bergson

We have forgotten that nature is us and that we are a manifestation of nature. When we treat nature as inanimate, without a soul, then we are dooming ourselves to all the suffering that stems from neglect of soul.

I can imagine a "natural spirituality," a religious sensibility rooted in nature. Nature's mysteries, vastness, and beauty offer an important grounding for spiritual vision and sensitivity. Without this grounding, evident in religious literature from around the world, our very spiritual lives become mostly mental and dangerously narcissistic. Nature is the beginning of spiritual wisdom and the irreplaceable matrix of the soul.

Thomas Moore

The best remedy for those who are afraid, lonely, or unhappy is to go outside, somewhere where they can be quiet, alone with the heavens, nature, and God. Because only then does one feel that all is as it should be and that God wishes to see people happy, amidst the simple beauty of nature.

Anne Frank

There are no temples or shrines among us save those of nature. . . . A God who is enrobed in filmy veils of cloud, there on the rim of the visible world where our Great-Grandfather Sun kindles his evening camp-fire; who rides upon the rigorous wind of the north, or breathes forth spirit upon fragrant southern airs, whose war canoe is launched upon majestic rivers and inland seas—such a God needs no lesser cathedral.

Ohiyesa

If the sight of the blue skies fills you with joy, if a blade of grass springing up in the fields has power to move you, if the simple things of nature have a message that you understand, rejoice, for your soul is alive.

Eleonora Duse

I believe in the cosmos. All of us are linked to the cosmos. Look at the sun: if there is no sun, then we cannot exist. So nature is my god. To me, nature is sacred; trees are my temples and forests are my cathedrals.

Mikhail Gorbachev

I believe in God, only I spell it Nature.

Frank Lloyd Wright

Night

During the day we dance along the surface of life, the world lit by the full radiance of the sun, but at night, the light softens and away the world fades, and we are left to look deep within to find another source of illumination and beauty. At night we slow down, we relax, we seek solace in closeness with our family, and we prepare to enter into the liminal world of sleep. At night we strip off our masks and let down our hair and seek personal comfort in intimate rituals. At night our world narrows down to the confines of a home, and smaller still, a bed, and our companions narrow down to our families, to our animals, to our lovers, or simply to ourselves. At night we confront our demons and talk to our angels and pray to our gods and listen to our souls. Henry Beston advises the spiritual seeker, "Learn to reverence night and to put away the vulgar fear of it, for, with the banishment of night from the experience of man, there vanishes as well a religious emotion, a poetic mood, which gives depth to the adventure of humanity."

I often think that the night is more alive and more richly colored than the day.

Vincent Van Gogh

No sight is more provocative of awe than is the night sky.

Llewelyn Powys

Night, the beloved. Night, when words fade and things come alive.
When the destructive analysis of day is done, and all that is truly
important becomes whole and sound again. When man reassembles
his fragmentary self and grows with the calm of a tree.

Antoine de Saint-Exupéry

Though my soul may set in darkness, it will rise in perfect light;
I have loved the stars too fondly to be fearful of the night.

Sarah Williams

Night's deepest gloom is but a calm; that soothes the weary mind:
The labored days restoring balm; the comfort of mankind.

Leigh Hunt

O wild and wondrous midnight,
There is a might in thee
To make the charmed body
Almost like spirit be,
And give it some faint glimpses
Of immortality.

James Russell Lowell

It seemed to be a necessary ritual that he should prepare himself
for sleep by meditating under the solemnity of the night sky . . .
a mysterious transaction between the infinity of the soul
and the infinity of the universe.

Victor Hugo

By night, an atheist half believes in God.

Edward Young

Then stars arise, and the night is holy.

Henry Wadsworth Longfellow

Come, drink the mystic wine of Night,
Brimming with silence and the stars;
While earth, bathed in this holy light,
Is seen without its scars.

Louis Untermeyer

 Science

A religion old or new, that stressed the magnificence of the universe
as revealed by modern science, might be able to draw forth reserves
of reverence and awe hardly tapped by the conventional faiths.
Sooner or later, such a religion will emerge.

Carl Sagan

Spirituality is a blanket term for the new religion that Carl Sagan believes will
eventually emerge. At its best, spirituality is inclusive of science, even wel-
coming, for exactly Sagan's reason—it understands that every scientific
discovery leads only to more reverence and awe for the universe, not less,
and that reverence and awe are two hallmarks of genuine spirituality. So
are curiosity, exploration, truth-seeking, wisdom, and wonder also characteristics of both science and spirituality. As Sagan notes, "Science is not
only compatible with spirituality; it is a profound source of spirituality."
If we take this statement as our hypothesis, we can try this as our experiment: to be more aware of our spirituality whenever and wherever we are
in the presence of science.

One [a scientist] is the educated man who still has a controlled sense of wonder before the universal mystery, whether it hides in a snail's eye or within the light that impinges on that delicate organ.

Loren Eiseley

Science cannot solve the ultimate mystery of nature because we ourselves are part of nature and therefore part of the mystery we are trying to solve.

Max Planck

Men love to wonder, and that is the seed of science.

Ralph Waldo Emerson

The more we learn of science, the more we see that its wonderful mysteries are all explained by a few simple laws so connected together and so dependent upon each other, that we see the same mind animating them all.

Olympia Brown

The religion that is afraid of science dishonors God and commits suicide.

Ralph Waldo Emerson

Equipped with his five senses, man explores the universe around him and calls the adventure Science.

Edwin Powell Hubble

The greatest discoveries of science have always been those that forced us to rethink our beliefs about the universe and our place in it.

Robert L. Park

Science and religion, religion and science, put it as I may, they are two sides of the same glass, through which we see darkly until these two, focusing together, reveal the truth.

Pearl Buck

Science without religion is lame, religion without science is blind.

Albert Einstein

Every formula which expresses a law of nature is a hymn of praise to God.

Maria Mitchell

Have no fear of natural science—it brings us nearer to God.

Albert Schweitzer

I do not believe in a personal God and I have never denied this but have expressed it clearly. If something is in me which can be called religious then it is the unbounded admiration for the structure of the world so far as our science can reveal it.

Albert Einstein

 ## The Seasons

When meeting someone new, I always ask what their favorite season is, and I'm no longer surprised at how firmly most people tend to respond, usually breaking it down into the season they adore, the other season that's nice too, the season they can't stand, and the season that's tolerable. Never has a person immediately replied with "Every one of them is my favorite! There is something amazing about them all!"—though when pressed in that direction, I know all of us could find at least one nice thing to say about each season.

Each season comes, bringing to us, and then goes, taking away from us, its own colors, smells, tastes, sights, activities, holidays, memories, weather, clothing, chores, and nothing short of lessons as eternal as birth, growth, aging, and death. Being in touch with our spirituality year-round means finding the spiritual beauty in each of the seasons as they pass. As a wise Wu-men wrote,

Ten thousand flowers in spring,
the moon in autumn,
a cool breeze in summer,
snow in winter.
If your mind isn't clouded by unnecessary things,
this is the best season of your life.

Beauty, in our eyes, is always fresh and living, even as God, the Great Mystery, dresses the world anew at each season of the year.

Ohiyesa

All seasons are beautiful for the person who carries happiness within.

Horace Friess

The seasons are what a symphony ought to be: four perfect movements in harmony with each other.

Arthur Rubinstein

To be interested in the changing seasons is a happier state of mind than to be hopelessly in love with spring.

George Santayana

Live in each season as it passes; breathe the air, drink the drink, taste the fruit, and resign yourself to the influences of each. Let them be your only diet drink and botanical medicines.

Henry David Thoreau

SPRING

If spring came but once a century instead of once a year, or burst forth with the sound of an earthquake and not in silence, what wonder and expectation there would be in all hearts to behold the miraculous change.

Henry Wadsworth Longfellow

Spring shows what God can do with a drab and dirty world.

Virgil A. Kraft

Spring—an experience in immortality.

Henry David Thoreau

We need spring. We need it desperately and, usually, we need it before God is willing to give it to us.

Peter Gzowski

Every spring is the only spring—a perpetual astonishment.

Ellis Peters

Our Lord has written the promise of the resurrection not in words alone, but in every leaf in springtime.

Martin Luther

SUMMER

That beautiful season the Summer!
Filled was the air with a dreamy and magical light;
and the landscape
Lay as if new created in all the freshness of childhood.

Henry Wadsworth Longfellow

I walk without flinching through the burning cathedral of the summer.
My bank of wild grass is majestic and full of music.
It is a fire that solitude presses against my lips.

Violette Leduc

Summer afternoon—summer afternoon; to me those have always
been the two most beautiful words in the English language.

Henry James

I should like to enjoy this summer flower by flower,
as if it were to be the last one for me.

André Gide

Summer is the time when one sheds one's tensions with one's
clothes, and the right kind of day is jeweled balm for the battered
spirit. A few of those days and you can become drunk with the
belief that all's right with the world.

Ada Louise Huxtable

FALL

Thy bounty shines in autumn unconfined
And spreads a common feast for all that live.

James Thomson

Delicious autumn! My very soul is wedded to it,
and if I were a bird I would fly about the earth
seeking the successive autumns.

George Eliot

Autumn is the eternal corrective. It is ripeness and color and a time of
maturity; but it is also breadth, and depth, and distance. What man can
stand with autumn on a hilltop and fail to see the span of his world
and the meaning of the rolling hills that reach to the far horizon?

Hal Borland

Autumn evening—
Knees in arms,
Like a saint.

Kobayashi Issa

In those vernal seasons of the year, when the air is calm and pleasant,
it were an injury and sullenness against Nature not to go out, and
see her riches, and partake in her rejoicing with heaven and earth.

John Milton

WINTER

The winter river;
down it come floating
flowers offered to Buddha.

Yosa Buson

How winter fills my soul!

Sylvia Plath

Winter is the time for comfort, for good food and warmth, for the touch of a friendly hand and for a talk beside the fire: it is the time for home.

Dame Edith Sitwell

Winter, a lingering season, is a time to gather golden moments, embark upon a sentimental journey, and enjoy every idle hour.

John Boswell

Winter teaches us about detachment, numbness. But it's a way to get through. From winter we learn silence and acceptance and the stillness thickens.

Gail Barison

The Sky and Its Bodies

"The sky is the soul of all scenery," Thomas Cole once said. "It makes the earth lovely at sunrise and splendid at sunset. In the one it breathes over the earth a crystal-like ether, in the other a liquid gold." If he's right in imagining the sky as the soul of all scenery, then it makes rightful sense why so many of us feel our souls drawn to the sky and the beautiful bodies that our naked eye daily and nightly can behold: the sun, the moon, and the stars. Abraham Lincoln wrote, "I never behold them [the heavens] that I do not feel I am looking into the face of God. I can see how it might be possible for a man to look down upon the earth and be an atheist, but I cannot conceive how he could look up into the heavens and say there is no God."

Connecting with our spirituality comes sometimes simply by looking up.

THE MOON

Moonlight is sculpture.

Nathaniel Hawthorne

Such a moon—
Even a thief
pauses to sing.

Buson

Not secondary to the sun, she gives us his blaze again,
Void of its flame, and sheds a softer day. . . .
In Heaven queen she is among the spheres;
She, mistresslike, makes all things to be pure.

Henry David Thoreau

There is something haunting in the light of the moon; it has all the
dispassionateness of a disembodied soul, and something of its
inconceivable mystery.

Joseph Conrad

The moon is a white strange world, great, white, soft-seeming globe in
the night sky, and what she actually communicates to me across space
I shall never fully know. But the moon that pulls the tides, and the moon
that controls the menstrual periods of women, and the moon that
touches the lunatics, she is not the mere dead lump of the astronomist.

D. H. Lawrence

Under the full moon life is all adventure.

Sigurd Olson

THE SKY

When you look up at the sky, you have a feeling of unity
which delights you and makes you giddy.

Ferdinand Hodler

Our passionate preoccupation with the sky, the stars, and a God
somewhere in outer space is a homing impulse. We are drawn
back to where we came from.

Eric Hoffer

When I was a boy, my eyes were open to the magic of the world. I knew
that if I jumped high enough, I could touch the sun, the moon, and
the stars. They belonged to me and I loved them.

William H. Thomas

The spectacle of the sky overwhelms me. I'm overwhelmed when I see
in an immense sky, the crescent of the moon, or the sun.

Joan Miró

The sky and the strong wind have moved the spirit inside me till
I am carried away trembling with joy.

Uvavnuk

The sky is the daily bread of the eyes.

Ralph Waldo Emerson

My soul is in the sky.

William Shakespeare

THE STARS

There they stand, the innumerable stars, shining in order
like a living hymn, written in light.

N. P. Willis

Silently, one by one, in the infinite meadows of heaven,
Blossomed the lovely stars, the forget-me-nots of the angels.

Henry Wadsworth Longfellow

Lift up my eyes from the earth and let me not forget the uses of the stars.

Max Ehrmann

When I have a terrible need of—shall I say the word—religion.
Then I go out and paint the stars.

Vincent Van Gogh

When I go out at night and look at all the stars in the sky, I feel the
power of the billions of stars and the enormous humility that comes
from being—I imagine—just one little speck of energy in a gigantic
infinity. I feel awed by the mystery of being both so finite and yet so
infinite, so much and so little, so conscious and yet, so coincidental.
For me, the massiveness of what I don't know creates one way
I experience God. It creates in me a feeling of humility and a
sense of gratitude for being given the gift of life.

Warren Farrell

So many people become so involved in televisions and radar that they've forgotten to think about the beautiful stars that bedeck the heavens like swinging lanterns of eternity, standing there like shining silvery pins sticking in the magnificent blue pincushion—something that man could never make.

Martin Luther King, Jr.

My mother told me that the stars—the few stars we could see—were windows into heaven. Windows for God to look through to keep an eye on us.

Octavia E. Butler

THE SUN

Give me the splendid silent sun
with all his beams full-dazzling.

Walt Whitman

The sun
Won a beauty contest and became a jewel
Set upon God's right hand.

Hafiz

Adore the Sun,
rising with all his rays,
receiving the obeisance
of gods and demons,
the shining maker of light.

the Ramayana

In sunlight, spirit streams to the earth, the spirit of love. . . .
Together with physical sunlight streams the warm love
of the Godhead for the earth.

Rudolf Steiner

The Sun, the hearth of affection and life,
pours burning love on the delighted earth.

Arthur Rimbaud

If you only knew the power, wealth, light, purity, and intelligence
contained in just one ray of sunlight! Yes, intelligence, too: does that
surprise you? I tell you, no one on earth, not even the greatest scientist
or the greatest genius, is as intelligent as a ray of sunlight!

Omraam Mikhaël Aïvanhov

Trees and Forests

Professor Christopher Witcombe, in writing about sacred places, notes
this about trees and forests: "From the earliest times, trees have been the
focus of religious life for many peoples around the world. As the largest
plant on earth, the tree has been a major source of stimulation to the
mythic imagination. Trees have been invested in all cultures with a dignity
unique to their own nature, and tree cults, in which a single tree or a
grove of trees is worshipped, have flourished at different times almost
everywhere. Even today there are sacred woods in India and Japan, just
as there were in pre-Christian Europe. An elaborate mythology of trees
exists across a broad range of ancient cultures."

Just two cultural references here will serve to remind us of the sacred
nature of trees. In the beginning, there were the two trees that played a
central place in Genesis's Garden of Eden: the Tree of Life and the Tree of

Knowledge of Good and Evil. In Buddhism, Prince Siddhartha achieved enlightenment while sitting under a tree, transforming him into Buddha (the Enlightened One) and the papal tree into the Bodhi tree (the Tree of Enlightenment). While we may not gain eternal life or achieve wisdom and enlightenment sitting under a tree or walking through a forest, we can surely come closer to our spiritual natures by contemplating and communing with the trees.

Did you know that trees talk? Well, they do. They talk to each other, and they'll talk to you if you listen. Trouble is, white people don't listen. They never learned to listen to the Indians so I don't suppose they'll listen to other voices in nature. But I have learned a lot from trees: sometimes about the weather, sometimes about animals, sometimes about the Great Spirit.

Tatanga Mani (Walking Buffalo)

Trees are the earth's endless effort to speak to the listening heaven.

Rabindranath Tagore

We have nothing to fear and a great deal to learn from trees, that vigorous and pacific tribe which without stint produces strengthening essences for us, soothing balms, and in whose gracious company we spend so many cool, silent, and intimate hours.

Marcel Proust

I love looking at you, hundred-year-old tree, loaded with shoots and boughs as though you were a stripling. Teach me the secret of growing old like you, open to life, to youth, to dreams, as somebody aware that youth and age are merely steps towards eternity.

Dom Hélder Câmara

Approaching a tree we approach a sacred being who can teach us about love and about endless giving. She is one of millions of beings who provide our air, our homes, our fuel, our books. Working with the spirit of the tree can bring us renewed energy, powerful inspiration, deep communion.

Druid tree lore

Of all man's works of art, a cathedral is greatest. A vast and majestic tree is greater than that.

Henry Ward Beecher

Whoever does not love trees, does not love God.

Elder Amphilochios of Patmos

The planting of trees is the least self-centered of all that we can do. It is a purer act of faith than the procreation of children.

Thornton Wilder

Trees are the teachers, revealers, containers, companions, and protectors of the sacred, and our relationship to them, whether we meet them gently in a forest or, muscled and equipped, cut them down for the price of lumber, touches on our deepest values, emotions, and sense of meaning. Divinity resides somehow in the marrow of a tree and in the sanctuary made of the overarching branches of an avenue or the columns of a grove or the mere umbrella of a tree's foliage. "Cleave a piece of wood," says Jesus in the Gospel of Thomas, "I am there."

Thomas Moore

The groves were God's first temple.

William Cullen Bryant

In the country it is as if every tree said to me, "Holy! Holy!"
Who can ever express the ecstasy of the woods?

Ludwig van Beethoven

 Water and Its Bodies

Lao Tzu and the Taoists often use water as an analogy for spirit. The way they see it, "Water is fluid, soft, and yielding. But water will wear away rock, which is rigid and cannot yield. As a rule, whatever is fluid, soft, and yielding will overcome whatever is rigid and hard. This is another paradox: What is soft is strong." Water, like spirit, is also beautiful, essential, cleansing, creative, and destructive. Water, like spirit, can purify, reflect, nourish, restore, and renew. Water, like spirit, can change form, can be solid or liquid, can steam or stream or evaporate or pool up or freeze or flow freely.

The beauty of water as a source of spirit is that it's available to all of us, whether we connect with it as it falls in the form of rain, or as we visit it embodied in a river, lake, ocean, sea, or stream, or as we drink it down into our bodies or surround ourselves with it in our baths and showers. Regardless of its form, we can recognize with Loren Eisley, "If there is magic on the planet, it is contained in the water."

RAIN

How beautiful is the rain!
After the dust and the heat,
In the broad and fiery street,
In the narrow lane,
How beautiful is the rain!

Henry Wadsworth Longfellow

Living creatures are nourished by food, and food is nourished
by rain; rain itself is the water of life, which comes from
selfless worship and service.

the Bhagavad Gita

Rain is grace; rain is the sky condescending to the earth;
without rain, there would be no life.

John Updike

Every dewdrop and raindrop had a whole heaven within it.

Henry Wadsworth Longfellow

I loved the rain as a child. I loved the sound of it on the leaves of trees
and roofs and windowpanes and umbrellas and the feel of it on my
face and bare legs. I loved the hiss of rubber tires on rainy streets and
the flip-flop of windshield wipers. I loved the smell of wet grass and
raincoats and shaggy coats of dogs. A rainy day was a special day for me
in a sense that no other kind of day was—a day when the ordinariness
of things was suspended with ragged skies drifting to the color of pearl
and dark streets turning to dark rivers of reflected light and even
people transformed somehow as the rain drew them closer by giving
them something to think about together, to take common shelter
from, to complain of and joke about in ways that made them more like
friends than it seemed to me they were on ordinary sunny days. But
more than anything, I think, I loved rain for the power it had to make
indoors seem snugger and safer and a place to find refuge in from
everything outdoors that was un-home, unsafe. I loved rain for
making home seem home more deeply.

Frederick Buechner

RIVERS

There's no music like a little river's . . . it takes the mind out of doors . . . and . . . sir, it quiets a man down like saying his prayers.

Robert Louis Stevenson

We let a river shower its banks with a spirit that invades the people living there, and we protect that river, knowing that without its blessings the people have no source of soul.

Thomas Moore

Rivers are magnets for the imagination, for conscious pondering and subconscious dreams, thrills, and fears. People stare into the moving water, captivated, as they are when gazing into a fire. What is it that draws and holds us? The rivers' reflections of our lives and experiences are endless. The water calls up our own ambitions of flowing with ease, of navigating the unknown. Streams represent constant rebirth. The waters flow in, forever new, yet forever the same; they complete a journey from beginning to end, and then they embark on the journey again.

Tim Palmer

A river seems a magic thing.
A magic, moving, living part of the very earth itself.

Laura Gilpin

I have never seen a river that I could not love. Moving water . . . has a fascinating vitality. It has power and grace and associations. It has a thousand colors and a thousand shapes, yet it follows laws so definite that the tiniest streamlet is an exact replica of a great river.

Roderick Haig-Brown

To trace the history of a river, or a raindrop, as John Muir would have done, is also to trace the history of the soul, the history of the mind descending and arising in the body. In both we constantly seek and stumble on divinity, which, like the cornice feeding the lake and the spring becoming a waterfall, feeds, spills, falls, and feeds itself over and over again.

Gretel Ehrlich

I've known rivers; I've known rivers ancient as the world and older than the flow of human blood in human veins. My soul has grown deep like the rivers.

Langston Hughes

To put your hands in a river is to feel the chords that bind the earth together.

Barry Lopez

The rivers are our brothers. They quench our thirst. They carry our canoes and feed our children. You must give to the rivers the kindness you would give to any brother.

Chief Seattle

SEA AND OCEAN

To me the sea is a continual miracle;
The fishes that swim—the rocks—the motion of the waves—the ships, with men in them,
What stranger miracles are there?

Walt Whitman

He that will learn to pray, let him go to sea.

George Herbert

To me, the sea is like a person—like a child that I've known a long time.
It sounds crazy, I know, but when I swim in the sea I talk to it.
I never feel alone when I'm out there.

Gertrude Ederle

The Greeks and others who imagined the ocean as divine were not
beneath us in sophistication, but ahead of us. If anything, we have lost
the one thing that would sustain our intimacy with nature—a religious
sensitivity to the sacredness of all forms in nature. The oceans are not
only a bountiful source of fish, transformation, and recreation; they
are also one of the supreme sources on the planet for contemplation
and other aspects of the spiritual life, but we could know this only
if we were deeply schooled in the necessary virtue of reverence.

Thomas Moore

My soul is full of longing
For the secret of the Sea,
And the heart of the great ocean
Sends a thrilling pulse through me.

Henry Wadsworth Longfellow

If there is poetry in my book about the sea, it is not because I
deliberately put it there, but because no one could write truthfully
about the sea and leave out the poetry.

Rachel Carson

WATER

The many waters I've known as part of my own personal world—rivers, streams, and lakes—have taught me, shaped me, and given me a sense of values. They have extended the process of transformation that began the day I was baptized, when a trickle of water flowed over the crown of my head and down its side, initiating me out of sheer physical existence into a life of alchemical, elemental, and religious change. Religion knows something of the mystery by which we become more human through our acquaintance with water.

Thomas Moore

By means of water, we give life to everything.

the Koran, 21:30

Water is the formless potential out of which creation emerged. It is the ocean of unconsciousness enveloping the islands of consciousness. Water bathes us at birth and again at death, and in between it washes away sin. It is by turns the elixir of life or the renewing rain or the devastating flood.

Scott Russell Sanders

We call upon the waters that rim the earth,
horizon to horizon, that flow in our rivers and streams,
that fall upon our gardens and fields,
and we ask that they teach us
and show us the way.

Chinook blessing

A man of wisdom delights in water.

Confucius

Water is also one of the four elements, the most beautiful of God's creations. It is both wet and cold, heavy, and with a tendency to descend, and flows with great readiness. It is this the Holy Scripture has in view when it says, "And the darkness was upon the face of the deep. And the Spirit of God moved upon the face of the waters." Water, then, is the most beautiful element and rich in usefulness, and purifies from all filth, and not only from the filth of the body but from that of the soul, if it should have received the grace of the Spirit.

John of Damascus

Here are your waters and your watering place.
Drink and be whole again beyond confusion.

Robert Frost

PEOPLE

To love another person is to see the face of God.

Victor Hugo

We cannot see God himself, but we can see him
as he has chosen to reveal himself in
[those] who inspire love in our hearts.

Ib'n al-Arabi

 Babies

Malidoma Somé, born to the Dagara of Burkina Faso in Africa, writes in his book *Of Water and the Spirit* about the special role of babies in his tribe. Each baby is seen as a spirit who has chosen to take on a body in order to carry out special projects in the world. While the baby is still in the womb, a special ceremony is held where the incoming soul takes on the voice of the mother and answers questions put to it by a priest, including where the soul is from, what gender it is, and why it has chosen to come here. The most important early relationship a baby will have is with its grandparents, who help remind the child of what it said in the womb in order to guide it toward fulfilling its purpose. That relationship is equally important to the grandparents, who are hungry for news from the world of spirit where soon they will return; babies are thought to be the purest form of communication from that spiritual world.

You don't have to be Dagaran to sense the spirituality emanating from babies. Says Marilyn Atteberry, "Holding my granddaughter, her fingers around my pinkie, her sixteen-hour-old eyes looking into mine, her mouth making tiny sucking sounds, is feeling the heart of the Divine." Nor do you have to be a grandparent; I remember looking into the still unfocused eyes of my nephew Hayden and wondering whether babies' eyes take awhile to focus on this material world they just entered because they are still focusing on the spiritual world they just left. When looking at, holding, touching, or smelling a baby, perhaps all of us sense we are looking at, holding, touching, and smelling the heart of the Divine.

Do not despair, every new born baby is a potential prophet.

R. D. Laing

Babies are bits of star-dust blown from the hand of God. Lucky the woman who knows the pangs of birth for she has held a star.

Larry Barretto

Because I have fewer judgments about them, I find it particularly easy to see God in babies. In India they take the darshan (spiritual blessings) of saints. I think we can have the darshans of babies and have a similar experience.

Joan Borysenko

It is no small thing that they, who are so fresh from God, love us.

Charles Dickens

Father asked us what was God's noblest work. Anna said men, but I said babies. Men are often bad; babies never are.

Louisa May Alcott

A baby is born with the need to be loved—and never outgrows it. Children are God's apostles, day by day sent forth to preach of love and hope and peace.

James Russell Lowell

Babies are necessary to grown-ups. A new baby is like the beginning of all things—wonder, hope, a dream of possibilities. In a world that is cutting down its trees to build highways, losing its earth to concrete . . . babies are almost the only remaining link with nature, with the natural world of living things from which we spring.

Eda J. Le Shan

A baby is God's opinion that the world should go on.

Carl Sandburg

The human baby, the human being, is a mosaic of animal and angel.

Jacob Bronowski

 Children

One lazy summer afternoon in the bookstore, I couldn't help but laugh out loud while perusing *205 Questions Children Ask About God, Heaven, and Angels.* Here are some of the most ticklish ones.

> If God made spiders, why do people squish them?
> Will God give children toys if they ask for them?
> Is there a McDonald's in heaven?
> Why is hell dark if they have fires?
> Why doesn't God just zap the bad people?
> Do angels watch television?
> How did Adam know what to name the animals?

While the book was about providing parents the answers to these questions their children might ask, the answers were far less charming than the questions themselves.

One Easter morning, while I was driving my four-year-old niece home from church, she looked out the window and asked me, "Aunt Jem, does God live in the sky?" Turning the question around, I replied, "What do you think, Hayley?" "I think he does," she replied, continuing to stare outside. "Then let's say good morning to God!" I suggested. We rolled down the windows and at the top of our lungs shouted, "Good morning, God! Have a nice day!"

Ralph Waldo Emerson noted, "We find delight in the beauty and happiness of children that makes the heart too big for the body." I didn't find the Divine in church that morning, but I found it later in the car with a child shouting greetings to God. To spend time with children, to delight in both their spirit and in the Divine Spirit, can make the heart burst out of the body and can resurrect the soul.

> The soul is healed by being with children.
>
> Fyodor Dostoyevsky

Children are a wonderful gift. . . . They have an extraordinary capacity to see into the heart of things and to expose sham and humbug for what they are.

Bishop Desmond Tutu

Children are natural Zen masters; their world is brand new in each and every moment.

John Bradshaw

God sends children to enlarge our hearts, and to make us unselfish and full of kindly sympathies and affections.

Mary Howitt

I love little children, and it is not a slight thing when they, who are fresh from God, love us.

Charles Dickens

Sometimes looking deep into the eyes of a child, you are conscious of meeting a glance full of wisdom. The child has known nothing yet but love and beauty. All this piled-up world knowledge you have acquired is unguessed at by her. And yet you meet this wonderful look that tells you in a moment more than all the years of experience have seemed to teach.

Hildegarde Hawthorne

Where children are, there is the golden age.

Novalis

Children are the hands by which we take hold of heaven.

Henry Ward Beecher

Know you what it is to be a child? It is to be something very different from the person of today. It is to have a spirit yet streaming from the waters of baptism; it is to believe in love, to believe in loveliness, to believe in belief; it is to be so little that the elves can reach to whisper in your ear; it is to turn pumpkins into coaches, and mice into horses, lowness into loftiness, and nothing into everything, for each child has its fairy godmother in its soul.

Francis Thompson

Of all the dear sights in the world, nothing is so beautiful as children when they are giving something. Any small thing they give. Children give the world to you. They open the world to you as if it were a book you'd never been able to read. But when a gift must be found, it is always some absurd little thing, passed on crooked . . . an angel looking like a clown. Children have so little that they can give, because they never know they have given you everything.

Margaret Lee Runbeck

There are no seven wonders of the world in the eyes of a child. There are seven million.

Walt Streightiff

The sound of children at play is the closest thing to God's own voice we shall ever hear.

Bill Geiss

 Community

In *The Re-Enchantment of Everyday Life,* Thomas Moore speculates about the exponential rise in people calling themselves "spiritual, not religious." "Today, many people frustrated with the inadequacies they see in mainstream religion express their love of spirituality and their disdain of religion. They want to address their spiritual concerns without being distracted and impeded by the politics of religion." But, he notes, there is a problem with this: They may be throwing out the baby with the bathwater. If religion is the bathwater, the babies they are throwing out with religion are tradition and community, both of which "offer a necessary grounding for the spiritual quest." Granted, he writes, they need "tradition and community liberated from belief and dogmatic coercion." But without tradition and community to guide the spiritual seeker, he or she can demonstrate "occasional narcissism and wandering."

Rudolfo Anaya writes, "To create the self is natural, but we must not forget we also belong to the community of souls." For those seeking to deepen their spirituality, it is imperative to do the work of soul-searching and self-creating, but it is important to balance the singular search with the companionship of a community of like-minded and spirited souls who can serve to both challenge and charge us, to both support and sustain us, and to both ground us and to give us wings to fly.

> When the second Buddha comes, [he] will not come as an individual but as a community.
>
> Thich Nhat Hanh

> On a very practical level, the greatest difficulty with spiritual techniques is remembering to practice them. For that, I find that community is important. If the people I interact with on a social level are following a similar path, we can remind each other of what our lives are about. Teachers can also be important, but, to a large extent, I think we can all be teachers to each other. Only five percent of us may be Masters, but there are thousands of us. We can serve as valuable reminders to each other.
>
> Peter Russell

We will go into the future as a single sacred community,
or we will all perish in the desert.

Thomas Berry

One of the most important aspects of group worship is that it is done
as a community. There's a basic human need to be in the company of
others, to connect in mind and heart and to work together toward
common goals. Though we may be worshipping in our own ways and
asking for purely self-oriented things, there is a comfort in doing it as
part of a larger team. Although many rituals we perform to enhance
our spiritual selves are done alone, it's not possible to be a completely
spiritual person by shutting away the rest of the world all of the time.

Shana Aborn

Our real place is community. Place is not nature, or man-made
objects, but community—a group or groups of people united by a
common endeavor and by love and trust. Wherever community
appears, spirit descends.

Louise Cowan

We have considered the depth of the world and the depth of our souls.
But we are only in a world through a community of men. And we can
discover our souls only through the mirror of those who look at us.
There is no depth of life without the depth of common life.

Paul Tillich

The religious community is essential, for alone our vision is too
narrow to see all that must be seen. Together, our vision widens
and strength is renewed.

Mark Morrison-Reed

The Way is long—
let us go together.
The Way is difficult—
let us help each other.
The way is joyful—
let us share it.
The way is ours alone—
let us go in love.
The way grows before us—
let us begin.

Zen invocation

We are all longing to go home to some place we have never been—a place half-remembered and half-envisioned we can only catch glimpses of from time to time. Community. Somewhere, there are people to whom we can speak with passion without having the words catch in our throats. Somewhere a circle of hands will open to receive us, eyes will light up as we enter, voices will celebrate with us whenever we come into our own power. Community means strength that joins our strength to do the work that needs to be done. Arms to hold us when we falter. A circle of healing. A circle of friends. Someplace where we can be free.

Starhawk

 Family

I have been pondering the question, What is it about family that connects us with spirituality? I mean, really, families are such a mixed bag of nuts, sometimes literally, and often we are the furthest away from our spirituality when we are nearest to our families. Yet family still has its hold on us, a deep, powerful, and sometimes mysteriously inexplicable hold that makes it akin to the spiritual.

And then I ran into a sentence by Simone Weil that helped explain the hold. "To be rooted is perhaps the most important and least recognized need of the human soul," she wrote. That's what families provide for us, regardless of any and all other areas where they are functional or dysfunctional: They give us roots for our soul.

If we're lucky, they give us wings for our spirits as well.

Family life is full of major and minor crises—the ups and downs of health, success, and failure in career, marriage, and divorce—and all kinds of characters. It is tied to places and events and histories. With all of these felt details, life etches itself into memory and personality. It's difficult to imagine anything more nourishing to the soul.

Thomas Moore

The desire to be and have a sister is a primitive and profound one that may have everything or nothing to do with the family a woman is born to. It is a desire to know and be known by someone who shares blood and body, history and dreams.

Elizabeth Fishel

Families will not be broken. Curse and expel them, send their children wandering, drown them in floods and fires, and old women will make songs of all these sorrows and sit in the porches and sing them on mild evenings.

Marilynne Robinson

A happy family is but an earlier heaven.

John Bowring

Family faces are magic mirrors. Looking at people who belong to us, we see the past, present, and future.

Gail Lumet Buckley

The diversity in the family should be the cause of love and harmony, as it is in music where many different notes blend together in the making of a perfect chord.

Baha'i scriptures

The family is one of nature's masterpieces.

George Santayana

A mother is a mother still,
The holiest thing alive.

Samuel Taylor Coleridge

A brother is a friend provided by nature.

Legouve Pere

You don't choose your family.
They are God's gift to you, as you are to them.

Bishop Desmond Tutu

A family is a place where minds come in contact with one another. If these minds love one another the home will be as beautiful as a flower garden. But if these minds get out of harmony with one another it is like a storm that plays havoc with the garden.

Buddha

Nobody can do for little children what grandparents do.
Grandparents sort of sprinkle stardust over the lives of children.

Alex Haley

The goodness of the father reaches higher than a mountain;
that of the mother goes deeper than the ocean.

Japanese proverb

Home is the one place in all this world where hearts are sure of each
other. It is the place of confidence. It is the place where we tear off
that mask of guarded and suspicious coldness which the world forces
us to wear in self-defense, and where we pour out the unreserved
communications of full and confiding hearts. It is the spot where
expressions of tenderness gush out without any sensation of
awkwardness and without any dread of ridicule.

Frederick W. Robertson

 Friends

In the Upaddha Sutta, Buddha's disciple Ananda comments about *kalyana-mitta,* translated as spiritual friendship. "This is half of the holy life, Lord: being a friend with admirable people, a companion with admirable people, a colleague with admirable people." Buddha corrects him, replying, "Don't say that, Ananda. Don't say that. Being a friend with admirable people, a companion with admirable people, a colleague with admirable people is actually the whole of the holy life."

Why did Buddha place so much emphasis on spiritual friendship? In the Sambodhi Sutta, he explains as he advises a group of monks, "If wanderers who are members of other sects should ask you, 'What, friend, are the prerequisites for the development of the wings to self-awakening?' you should answer, 'There is the case where a monk has admirable people as friends, companions, and colleagues. This is the first prerequisite for the development of the wings to self-awakening.'" Buddha knew that friendship, like any relationship, offers the opportunity for self-awakening, or what we in the West might call "personal growth." Buddhist monk and teacher Ajahn Amaro describes it like this: "In spiritual friendship, we can actually be with each other. We open ourselves to the other person, ready to notice any grudges that we have, or the opinions and obsessions we have about them, as well as the attractions towards them. Then we can enter more into the place of listening, of forgiving, of letting go of the past and just being open to the present. And this is the most wonderful and beautiful gift we can give."

I think of Jesus' giving that gift to his disciples-turned-friends at the Last Supper, and then the words of Martin Buber come to mind: "When two people relate to each other authentically and humanly, God is the electricity that surges between them." What beautiful definitions of friendship from two very different traditions: the electricity of God, and the whole of the holy life.

A friend is called a guardian of love or, as some would have it,
a guardian of the spirit itself.

Saint Aelred of Rievaulx

The truth is friendship is every bit as sacred and eternal as marriage.

Katherine Mansfield

A soul friend is someone with whom we can share our greatest joys and
deepest fears, confess our worst sins and most persistent faults, clarify
our highest hopes and perhaps most unarticulated dreams.

Edward C. Sellner

Friendship . . . is an Union of Spirits, a Marriage of Hearts, and the Bond thereto Virtue.

William Penn

Some people go to priests; others to poetry; I to my friends.

Virginia Woolf

If you open the door to the magnetic power of friendship, souls of like vibrations will be attracted to you.

Paramahansa Yogananda

Friendship and loyalty are an identity of souls seldom found on earth. The only really lasting and valuable friendship is between people of a similar nature.

Gandhi

The essence of friendship is entireness, a total magnanimity and trust. It must not surmise or provide for infirmity. It treats its object as a god, that it may deify both. . . . Friendship demands a religious treatment. We talk of choosing our friends, but friends are self-elected. Reverence is a great part of it. Treat your friend as a spectacle.

Ralph Waldo Emerson

Friendship is a single soul dwelling in two bodies.

Aristotle

And let there be no purpose in friendship save the deepening of the spirit.

Kahlil Gibran

Spirit Guides

In her book on the Buddhist goddess of compassion, *Discovering Kwan Yin,* Sandy Boucher writes about how she came to be so influenced by the goddess. "Initially, I did not come easily to the idea of 'goddesses.' After all, I was a rational, politically active person who believed in the struggle for social change and avoided any religious contamination. The last thing I needed was a divine figure, of either gender, to show me the way. But gradually over the years, as the energy of Kwan Yin began to become real in my life, I had to give up my skepticism and begin to articulate for myself what the female sacred manifestations might actually be." She wrestles with whether Kwan Yin is a real "independent entity in the universe," or whether she exists only in the minds and hearts of those who need her guidance. Ultimately she says she's open to both interpretations, that what's more important is that Kwan Yin manifests herself in whatever form can be recognized by each person individually.

Many people who seek to explore the depths of their spirituality will find that a divine figure can act as guardian and guide. In the original Greek, *angelos* means messenger. An angel or any divine spirit acts as a messenger, an intermediary, a medium between the world of the human and the Divine. There are no limits to its manifestations: It can be a tree whose spirit speaks to you, or a bird that visits outside your window, or the spirit of an ancestor who guides you. It can be a fairy, a deva, a saint, a historical figure, or a religious one. It could be an image, a statue, a painting, a place, or simply the sensation of the presence of something beyond this material world. When we speak of these guiding spirits, we speak in the language of poetry, of imagination, of myth, of symbolism, and it matters less whether these things really exist than it does that they exist for us.

To forget one's ancestors is to be a brook without a source,
a tree without a root.

Chinese proverb

The fact that angels are included in religious traditions of every variety all over the world and that they have been painted by a multitude of artists, who portray their characteristics with remarkable consistency, is enough to convince me that angels are real and are to be taken seriously. I need no further proof, because sacred imagery is a more reliable source for the nature of religious experience than any scientific investigation or personal testimony.

Thomas Moore

The belief in guardian or guide spirits originated in tribal cultures. The spirit, usually in an animal form, protects individuals, tribes, clans, or provides some sort of magical shamanic power. The power possessed by the animal is generally believed to represent the collective power of the entire species or genus, giving the animal magical abilities to perform extraordinary feats, such as the wolf with the power to fight.

From the tribal viewpoint most Westerners still have guardian spirits, but are not aware of them throughout their lives. This is because of their lost contact with nature, and thus they rob themselves of this source of greater reinforcing power.

Alan G. Hefner

Throughout time human beings have recognized and honored their own divine nature through acknowledgement of spirit beings. . . . Spirit beings may be angels and guides, animal spirits, or the souls of trees. They protect and direct us in our daily lives. They bring comfort and wisdom. Perhaps more important, though, they enlarge our view of the Beyond and bring perspective. We become aware that we are part of something wonderful and mysterious, something bottomless and vast.

Nicole Marcelis

"If you knew who walked beside you at all times on this path that you have chosen, you could never experience fear again." The higher part of yourself has a "knowing" that you're not alone, that you go where you're sent, that you'll be guided, that you can surrender, and that it's going to work out.

Wayne Dyer

In the old Celtic imaginings, a person was born through three forces: the coming together of mother and father, an ancestral spirit's wish to be reborn, and the involvement of a god or goddess.

Michael Meade

Some souls have learned everything from invisible guides, known only to themselves. . . . The ancient sages taught that for each individual soul, or perhaps for a number of souls with the same nature and affinity, there is a being of the spiritual world, who, thorough their existence, adopts a special solicitude and tenderness toward that soul or group of souls: it is he who initiates them into knowledge, protects, guides, defends, comforts them.

Abu'l Barakat

From the tribal view point most Westerners still have guardian spirits, but are not aware of them throughout their lives. This is because of their lost contact with nature, and thus they rob themselves of this source of greater reinforcing power.

Alan G. Hefner

There is a deep need in the world just now for guidance—almost any sort of spiritual guidance.

Carl Jung

I experience God through the help of my allies. In the study of shamanism as I have learned it from the Sisterhood of the shields, "allies" are energy forms that give us strength and help. They also encourage and protect us. Different religions and cultures have given these energies different names, from leprechauns and angels to guwawas or little green men. Performing ceremonies in which I ask these energies to come in is another way I encounter the Great Spirit.

Lynne Andrews

THE
SENSUAL WORLD

Nothing can cure the soul but the senses,
just as nothing can cure the senses but the soul.

Oscar Wilde

We live on the leash of our senses.

Diane Ackerman

Art

In the Christian creation story, God looked out over the black, formless void that was the earth and he said, "Let there be light." On the great canvas of the earth's surface, he painted day and night, sky and seas, plants and trees, planets and stars, and finally, animals and humans, and he spun the color palate over all of them by creating the seasons with their ever-changing tones. Our genesis was a work of art done by the hands of the Great Creator.

If it is true that we were made in the image of that creator, it is of little wonder that we are constantly creating art ourselves. Artist and critic John Ruskin thought that "all great art is the expression of man's delight in God's work, not his own." We create art to reflect the beauty of the soul of the world in all of its seasons: the delight of spring, the zeal of summer, the mellowing of fall, and the despair of winter. Sometimes we create art to express our souls, sometimes to touch the souls of others, and sometimes to reflect and praise the work of God, but regardless of our motivations, the soul is always present when we create art.

Not everything has a name. Some things lead us into a realm beyond words. . . . By means of art we are sometimes sent—dimly, briefly— revelations unattainable by reason.

Aleksandr Solzhenitsyn

The whole notion of Tibetan art is that the act of creation is an act of worship, bringing merit to the artist.

Michael Tobias

Life beats down and crushes the soul, and art reminds you that you have one.

Stella Adler

Art is the conversation between lovers.
Art offers an opening for the heart.
True art makes the divine silence in the soul
Break into applause.

Hafiz

The primary benefit of practicing any art, whether well or badly,
is that it enables one's soul to grow.

Kurt Vonnegut

Art is the essence of awareness.

Louise Nevelson

A museum or a gallery is truly a temple in which the mysteries that I
have to deal with every day are presented for my reflection and deep
education. . . . When we make our pilgrimage to the museum, we find
images showing what the soul is made of, what my soul is made of. We
celebrate those artists who powerfully and beautifully pain the secret
sources of our lives. The images, so carefully made, educate our
imagination in the precision, depth, range, and focus of human life.
In a museum we see more of our souls than we could find through
any means of introspective analysis.

Thomas Moore

We seem to have lost contact with the earlier, more profound
functions of art, which have always had to do with personal and
collective empowerment, personal growth, communion with this
world, and the search for what lies beneath and above this world.

Peter London

The highest art is always the most religious, and the greatest artist is always a devout person.

Professor Blackie

Love is the only thing that is causeless, that is free; it is beauty, it is skill, it is art. Without love there is no art. When the artist is playing beautifully there is no "me," there is love and beauty, and this is art.

Krishna

Whether it's a pebble in a riverbed or a soaring mountain peak, I see everything in the world as the handiwork of the Lord. When I paint, I try to represent the beauty of God's creation in my art. Many modern painters see the world as a jumble of random lines and shapes with no divine beauty or order, and their works reflect their viewpoint. Because I see God's peacefulness, serenity, and contentment, I work to capture those feelings on the canvas. My vision of God defines my vision of the world.

Thomas Kinkade

All art is the expression of one and the same thing—the relation of the spirit of man to the spirit of other men and to the world.

Ansel Adams

We have no word for art. We do everything as beautifully as we can.

Balinese saying

 Beauty

I am haunted by the song "A Thousand Beautiful Things" from Annie Lennox's CD *Bare*. It has a hold on me the way a perfect song will; you not only listen to it constantly, but you also find the silence upon awakening is replaced with the refrain in your head, where you find your mind mulling over the rest of the lyrics the rest of the day. She sings of how difficult it sometimes is to see that "the glass is full and not half empty." Yet every day she reminds herself that there exist a thousand beautiful things, and remembering this, she sings, "I never want to close my eyes again."

In a world sometimes dark, sometimes ugly, we too can sing of the need for beauty in our lives. Poet Kahlil Gibran says beauty is more than a need; it is ecstasy, "a heart enflamed and a soul enchanted." We must keep our eyes open to find those thousand beautiful things that enflame and enchant our souls, for in the words of Joseph Addison, "There is nothing that makes its way more directly to the soul than beauty."

Whenever I experience something beautiful, I am with Soul. That moment of inward breath, that pause and awareness of "how beautiful this is" is a prayer of appreciation, a moment of gratitude in which I beheld beauty and am one with it. I have come to appreciate that having an aesthetic eye takes me effortlessly into soul.

Jean Shinoda Bolen

In all ranks of life the human heart yearns for the beautiful; and the beautiful things that God makes are his gift to all alike.

Harriet Beecher Stowe

Beauty will save the world.

Fyodor Dostoyevsky

Beauty is one of the rare things that do not lead to doubt of God.

Jean Anouilh

A man should hear a little music, read a little poetry, and see a fine picture every day of his life, in order that worldly cares may not obliterate the sense of the beautiful which God has implanted in the human soul. Beauty is an all-pervading presence. It unfolds to the numberless flowers of the Spring; it waves in the branches of the trees and in the green blades of grass; it haunts the depths of the earth and the sea, and gleams out in the hues of the shell and the precious stone.

And not only these minute objects, but the ocean, the mountains, the clouds, the heavens, the stars, the rising and the setting sun all overflow with beauty. The universe is its temple; and those people who are alive to it can not lift their eyes without feeling themselves encompassed with it on every side.

Johann Wolfgang von Goethe

Never lose an opportunity of seeing anything that is beautiful, for beauty is God's handwriting—a wayside sacrament. Welcome it in every fair face, in every fair sky, in every flower, and thank God for it as a cup of blessing.

Ralph Waldo Emerson

Everybody needs beauty as well as bread, places to play in and pray in, where Nature may heal and cheer and give strength to body and soul alike.

John Muir

God scatters beauty as he scatters flowers
O'er the wide earth, and tells us all are ours.
A hundred lights in every temple burn,
And at each shrine I bend my knee in turn.

Walter Savage Landor

 The Body

One of novelist D. H. Lawrence's themes was the power, the joy, and the beauty of the flesh and of all appetites that come from the body. In this celebration of embodiment, he was attempting to reverse a trend of many religious and spiritual systems that taught that the flesh was vile and the body's appetites were to be transcended. He wrote, "What man most passionately wants is his living wholeness and his living unison, not his own isolate salvation of his 'soul.' Man wants his physical fulfillment first and foremost, since now, once and once only, he is in the flesh and potent. For man, the vast marvel is to be alive. For man, as for flower and beast and bird, the supreme triumph is to be most vividly, most perfectly alive. Whatever the unborn and the dead may know, they cannot know the beauty, the marvel of being alive in the flesh. The dead may look after the afterwards. But the magnificent here and now of life in the flesh is ours, and ours alone, and ours only for a time. We ought to dance with rapture that we should be alive and in the flesh, and part of the living, incarnate cosmos." In Lawrence's thinking, the body is not merely a vehicle for spirit, but is a manifestation of spirit itself, and thus, when we nurture, honor, and feed the body its passions and pleasures, it cannot be separated from nurturing, honoring, and feeding the spirit as well.

A healthy perception of our bodies is one in which we surrender them to the Holy Spirit and ask that they be used as instruments through which love is expressed in the world.

Marianne Williamson

Here in this body are the sacred rivers: here are the sun and moon as well as all the pilgrimage places. . . . I have not encountered another temple as blissful as my own body.

Saraha

The body a tree,
God a wind.

Hafiz

The first thing people need to do in forming a deeper relationship
with God is open the energy channels inside themselves. The body
is a temple of God. If you want to make a connection with the Tao,
with God, you have to open the energy blockages within yourself.
That helps make your body a conductor for God's energy.

Mantak Chia

This body of yours is like a curriculum in school, only this is your
curriculum to God. This is your house of God, and it is in this body,
while it is here on this planet, that God can be realized. To find
anything about this house of God to be vile or disgusting is to sully the
temple that is the one place in the universe where you know you can
realize God. . . . You are privileged to have the body you have. Honor
it as if it is the garage in which you park your soul. Refuse to have
contemptuous thoughts about your soul's garage, your body.

Wayne Dyer

The body is a sacred garment.

Martha Graham

Your body is precious. It is our vehicle for awakening. Treat it with care.

Buddha

If anything is sacred the human body is sacred.

Walt Whitman

The body is a vehicle through which I become an
aesthetic expression of the self.

Tu Wei-Ming

Begin by working to heal your spirit. A healthy spirit is essential for a
healthy body, although a healthy spirit does not *guarantee* a healthy
body. Understanding your spirit does hold the key to helping control
what happens to your body and within it, however. Since many
complementary medical treatments require you to be conscious
of the role of the spirit in healing, you have to take personal steps
to unite that belief and spirit with your body. In short, you need
to physicalize your spirit, to embody it.

Carolyn Myss

Christ has no body now on earth but yours,
No hands but yours,
No feet but yours,
Yours are the eyes through which he is to look out
Christ's compassion to the world
Yours are the feet with which he is to go about doing good;
Yours are the hands with which he is to bless men now.

Teresa of Avila

 # Color

In Alice Walker's novel *The Color Purple,* Shug explains her vision of God
to Celie. "God is inside you and inside everybody else. You come into this
world with God. . . . I believe God is everything. Everything that is or ever
was or ever will be." Then she explains to Celie, "People think pleasing

God is all God care about. But any fool living in the world can see it always trying to please us back." God loves admiration, she tells her, and loves sharing the good things in the world. She says, "I think it pisses God off if you walk by the color purple in a field somewhere and don't notice it."

God, Shug explains, is "always making little surprises and springing them on us when us least expect." Color is one of those surprises. Surrounded by color, we are surrounded by spirit, and "mere color, unspoiled by meaning, and unallied with definite form, can speak to the soul in a thousand different ways" (Oscar Wilde). If color is God's way of speaking to the soul, then we are always being spoken to—whether it's by the majesty of the color purple in a field or by the ordinariness of a child's box of crayons.

Of all God's gifts to the sighted man, color is holiest,
the most divine, the most solemn.

John Ruskin

Color is the language of the poets. It is astonishingly lovely.
To speak it is a privilege.

Keith Crown

Color! What a deep and mysterious language, the language of dreams.

Paul Gauguin

The whole world, as we experience it visually, comes to us through
the mystic realm of color. Our entire being is nourished by it.

Hans Hofmann

The world speaks to me in colours, my soul answers in music.

Rabindranath Tagore

Some of us come on earth seeing—some of us come on earth seeing color.

Louise Nevelson

We are all at different stages of growth, so we each need different things to trigger that connection to the soul. What works for me on any given day might not work for someone else, or for me on another day. Often, it is the basic things. I live ten feet from the ocean, in a small cottage. I need to be by the water; I've spent a lot of my journey getting closer and closer to this water. I need to remember, to get up in the morning and watch the sunrise and take a moment at night to see and feel the sunset. I need to see the colors of the sky; I need to feel the colors. I need to surround myself with music, because my soul resonates to music. I've decorated my home with the colors of the universe—bright colors. Color is light. Colors help me feel alive, help me feel passionate, help me remember that I'm here to be an alive, passionate human being.

Melody Beattie

Color possesses me. There is no need to seize it. It possesses me. I know. Here is the meaning of the happy moment: color and I are one.

Paul Klee

Among the several kinds of beauty, the eye takes most delight in colors.

Joseph Addison

Color is like food for the spirit—plus it's not addictive or fattening.

Isaac Mizarani

We were always intoxicated with color, with words that speak of color, and with the sun that makes colors live.

Andre Derain

Color is the keyboard, the eyes are the harmonies,
the soul is the piano with many strings.

Wassily Kandinsky

Food and Wine

The Bible says, "A man hath no better thing under the sun, than to eat, and to drink, and to be merry." Certainly food and wine serve many purposes, like nourishing our bodies, like providing creature comfort and joy, like teasing and pleasing our senses; they also serve the purpose of powerfully lifting and reviving our spirits, connecting us as well with the spirit of the earth, the sun, the seed, the wind, and the water, the toil and the sweat that came together to create the blessings we know as food and wine.

FOOD

Food to a large extent is what holds a society together and eating
is closely linked to deep spiritual experiences.

Peter Farb and George Armelagos

Food responds to our soul's dream as to our stomach's appetite.

Joseph Delteil

Food . . . can look beautiful, taste exquisite, smell wonderful, make
people feel good, bring them together, inspire romantic feelings. . . .
At its most basic, it is fuel for a hungry machine.

Rosamond Richardson

Food is our common ground, a universal experience.

James Beard

To the ruler, the people are heaven; to the people, food is heaven.

Chinese proverb

If a man be sensible and one fine morning, while he is lying in bed,
count at the tips of his fingers how many things in this life truly will
give him enjoyment, invariably he will find food is the first one.

Lin Yutang

But eventually there is no god who can keep us from tasting.

Hélène Cixous

Food is the most primitive form of comfort.

Sheila Graham

All food is the gift of the gods and has something of the miraculous,
the egg no less than the truffle.

Sybille Bedford

The act of putting into your mouth what the earth has grown is
perhaps your most direct interaction with the earth.

Frances Moore Lappe

God comes to the hungry in the form of food.

Gandhi

WINE

Wine is the pleasantest subject in the world to discuss. All its associations are with occasions when people are at their best; with relaxation, contentment, leisurely meals, and the free flow of ideas.

Hugh Johnson

We hear of the conversion of water into wine at the marriage in Cana as of a miracle. But this conversion is, through the goodness of God, made every day before our eyes. Behold the rain which descends from heaven upon our vineyards, and which incorporates itself with the grapes, to be changed into wine; a constant proof that God loves us, and loves to see us happy.

Benjamin Franklin

If food is the body of good living, wine is its soul.

Clifton Fadiman

Nothing more excellent or valuable than wine
was ever granted by the gods to man.

Plato

Good wine carrieth a man to heaven.

Anglo-Saxon saying

There is nothing like wine for conjuring up feelings of contentment and goodwill. It is less of a drink than an experience, an evocation, a spirit. It produces sensations that defy description.

Thomas Conklin

One barrel of wine can work more miracles than a church full of saints.

Italian proverb

Wine opens the heart. It warms the shy poet hidden in the cage of the ribs. It melts the wax in the ears that music may be heard. It takes the terror from the tongue that truth may be said, or what rhymes marvelously with truth. The soft warm sting on the cheekbones that a ripe Burgundy gives is only the thin outward pervasion of a fine heat within, when the cruel secret smolder of the wit leaps into clear flame, flame that consumes the sorry rubbish of precaution and cajolery.

Christopher Morley

When we drink, we get drunk. When we get drunk, we fall asleep. When we fall asleep, we commit no sin. When we commit no sin, we go to heaven. Sooooo, let's all get drunk, and go to heaven . . .

Brian O'Rourke

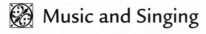 Music and Singing

Humanity. A musical instrument for God.

When I first read this simple statement from Thomas Merton, I immediately wondered, "Well then, what kind of musical instrument am I? Am I a flute, airy and soft? Am I a piano, black and white? Am I a cello, deep and resonant? Or am I just a cymbal, walking around banging against myself making big noise?" And then I asked, "Am I sharp? Am I flat? Am I in rhythm? Am I off-key? How's my volume? Do I ever make you want to stand up and dance, shake your skin loose? Am I ever so soothing I lull you to sleep?"

When I stopped having fun with all the questions (try them, they really *are* fun!), I began to think of the enchanting and enhancing function of music on our spirits. Though we experience it to differing degrees, I can't imagine anyone who is truly alive who hasn't had the experience of music that "lifts their spirits" and "takes them to another world," whether it's listening to music, composing or creating it, or through playing or singing. And perhaps Merton is on to the reason why—when the human instrument gets hold of the musical instrument, what plays or sings is God.

There is something very wonderful in music. Words are wonderful enough; but music is even more wonderful. It speaks not to our thoughts as words do; it speaks straight to our hearts and spirits, to the very core and root of our souls. Music soothes us, stirs us up; it puts noble feelings in us; it melts us to tears; we know not how; it is a language by itself, just as perfect, in its way, as speech, as words; just as divine, just as blessed.

Charles Kingsley

The Spirit speaks directly to our hearts through music. That's why music has always had such power to move people into positive action.

Kenny Loggins

I am
A hole in a flute
That the Christ's breath moves through—
Listen to this
Music.

Hafiz

Music is the divine way to tell beautiful, poetic things to the heart.

Pablo Casals

Yet there is one thing the world with all its rottenness cannot take from us, and that is the deep abiding joy and consolation perpetuated in great music. Here the spirit may find home and relief when all else fails.

Eric Fenby

Listening to great music is a shattering experience, throwing the soul into an encounter with an aspect of reality to which the mind cannot ever relate itself adequately. Such experiences undermine conceit and complacency and even induce a sense of contrition and a readiness for repentance. I am neither a musician nor an expert on music. But the shattering experience of music has been a challenge to my thinking on ultimate issues. I spend my life working with thoughts. And one problem that gives me no rest is: do these thoughts ever rise to the heights reached by authentic music?

Abraham Joshua Heschel

Music is well said to be the speech of angels; in fact, nothing among the utterances allowed to man is felt to be so divine. It brings us near to the infinite.

Thomas Carlyle

What a divine calling is music! Though everything else may appear shallow and repulsive, even the smallest task in music is so absorbing, and carries us so far away from town, country, earth, and all worldly things, that it is truly a blessed gift of God.

Felix Mendelssohn

All true and deeply felt music, whether sacred or profane, journey to heights where art and religion can always meet.

Albert Schweitzer

Music comes before religion, as emotion comes before thought, and sound before sense. What is the first thing you hear when you go into a church? The organ playing.

Alfred North Whitehead

Music is to the other arts, considered as a whole, what religion is to the church. There is nothing better than music as a means for uplifting the soul.

Hazrat Inayat Khan

We need magic, and bliss, and power, myth, and celebration and religion in our lives, and music is a good way to encapsulate a lot of it.

Jerry Garcia

Music can be all things to all persons. It is like a great dynamic sun in the center of a solar system which sends out its rays and inspiration in every direction. Music makes us feel that the heavens open and a divine voice calls. Something in our souls responds and understands.

Leopold Stokowski

There is nothing in the world so much like prayer as music is.

William P. Merrill

Music, my joy, my full-scale God.

Gwen Harwood

SINGING

The human voice is the organ of the soul.

Henry Wadsworth Longfellow

What interested me was that music is the most specific language that exists. It can say things that no other language has words for. It can put its finger on moments of human feeling that go largely unacknowledged in a verbally dominated culture like our own, where for most people the only reality is a verbal reality. . . . Most people's lives are, again and again, reduced to what they can talk about. And that's a very narrow band of the world! The time you spend with music is time spent in that larger realm. . . . The point about opera is that song is the one thing that connects all human beings. Words, again and again, divide us. Song, again and again, brings us together. The voice goes so deep and connects to breathing, to what makes us alive.

In that regard, vocal music is an attempt to take the whole human being and project it into space. It is the ultimate gesture of getting out of yourself. You take the one part of you that is most private, most personal, most inward, and you hurl it out into space, you project it as far as you can. That gesture of opening this whole region of the body results in a tremendous spiritual release, and is felt by other people with tremendous impact.

Peter Sellars

A singer starts by having his instrument as a gift from God. . . . When you have been given something in a moment of grace, it is sacrilegious to be greedy.

Marian Anderson

God sent his Singers upon earth
With songs of sadness and of mirth,
That they might touch the hearts of men,
And bring them back to heaven again.

Henry Wadsworth Longfellow

Since I felt that I wasn't getting anywhere [getting closer to God] on my own, a spiritual teacher had to tell me what would be helpful to try. He told me to sing devotional songs to God—a practice I thought was "beneath me." As a highly intellectual person, I viewed the idea of singing songs to God as very embarrassing. Lo and behold, around the third or fourth time I tried, I was suddenly overwhelmed with feelings of love, bliss, and joy! This experience taught me that I don't always know what's best for me. Nowadays, people can't stop me from singing.

Jonathan Robinson

With my song will I praise Him.

Psalms 28:7

The body is truly the garment of the soul, which has a living voice; for that reason it is fitting that the body, simultaneously with the soul, repeatedly sings praises to God through the voice.

Hildegard von Bingen

I am grateful that I have a spirit inside me which often sings.

Nina Holton

 # Poetry

Do you remember Robin Williams' playing John Keating in the movie *The Dead Poets Society*? Inspiring his young students toward a love of poetry, he tells them, "We don't read and write poetry because it's cute. We read and write poetry because we are members of the human race and the human race is filled with passion. Medicine, law, business, engineering, these are noble pursuits and necessary to sustain life. But poetry, beauty, romance, love, these are what we stay alive for. To quote from Whitman, 'O me! O life! Of the questions of these recurring, of the endless trains of the faithless, of cities filled with the foolish; what good amid these, O me, O life? Answer. That you are here, that life exists, and identity; that the powerful play goes on and you may contribute a verse.' That the powerful play goes on and you may contribute a verse. What will your verse be?"

Whether you contribute your own verse, or appreciate the powerful play that goes on in the poetry of another, poetry is one of the lightning-flash ways to electrify, beautify, dignity, and inspire the spirit. In the words of the poet Hafiz,

A poet is someone
Who can pour light into a cup,
Then raise it to nourish
Your beautiful parched, holy mouth.

Poetry is the voice of the soul, whispering, celebrating, singing even.

Carolyn Forché

My poems are hymns of praise to the glory of life.

Dame Edith Sitwell

Poetry, my dear friends, is a sacred incarnation of a smile. Poetry is a sigh that dries the tears. Poetry is a spirit who dwells in the soul, whose nourishment is the heart, whose wine is affection. Poetry that comes not in this form is a false messiah.

Kahlil Gibran

Poetry proceeds from the totality of man, sense, imagination, intellect, love, desire, instinct, blood, and spirit together.

Jacques Maritain

Ink runs from the corners of my mouth.
There is no happiness like mine.
I have been eating poetry.

Mark Strand

Poetry reveals to us the loveliness of nature, brings back the freshness
of youthful feelings, reviews the relish of simple pleasures, keeps
unquenched the enthusiasm which warmed the springtime of
our being, refines youthful love, strengthens our interest in
human nature, by vivid delineations of its tenderest and softest
feelings, and through the brightness of its prophetic visions,
helps faith to lay hold on the future life.

William E. Channing

The
Great religions are the
Ships,
Poets the life
Boats.

Hafiz

 Scent

More so than religions practiced in the West, Eastern religions and spiritual systems have long recognized the power of scent to evoke spirituality.
Peg Streep writes, "The use of incense—originally burned gums or resins—
in religious ceremonies is universal and ancient in its origins. Though
incense was used for its fumigatory and cleansing power, it also played,
as it continues to, an important symbolic role in ritual observance. The
perfume released by the incense symbolized the active presence of a

higher spirit, god, or goddess, while the smoke wafting up from the incense represented prayers, thus bridging the gap between the earthly and the spiritual." Besides incense, flower essences and oils have also been used to evoke and invoke the Divine; Western culture is catching on to this connection, particularly as it deals with healing, through the popularity of aromatherapy. Though we'd be hard-pressed to say what we mean by it, who hasn't walked by a flower shop or through a kitchen alive with scent and commented, "That smells divine"?

Smell is a potent wizard that transports us across thousands of miles and all the years we have lived.

Helen Keller

The smell and taste of things remain poised a long time, like souls, ready to remind us.

Marcel Proust

In Hebrew, the words *spirituality* and *fragrance* have a shared grammatical origin and are therefore almost identical: the word for "spirit" is *Ruach* and for "scent" is *Reach*. This reflects the ancient belief that sanctity is characterized by divine fragrance.

Dr. Naomie Poran

The fragrance of holiness travels even against the wind.

Buddha

When I was a boy, I thought scent was contained in dewdrops on flowers and if I got up very early in the morning, I could collect it and make perfume.

Oscar de la Renta

Through the frequent use of plants and things that are alive you can take a great deal from the spirit of the world, and especially if you nourish and strengthen yourself either with living things or with things only recently rooted in mother earth. Also, as much as possible you should be among plants that smell sweet or at least not bad. All herbs, flowers, trees, and fruits are aromatic, even though we may not always notice it. By means of this fragrance, as though it were the breath and spirit of the world's vitality, they nourish you and refresh you. Indeed, I would say that your own spirit is very much like these fragrances, and through this spirit, the link between your body and soul, these fragrances refresh your body and wonderfully restore your soul.

Marsilio Ficino

Nothing revives the past so completely as a smell that was once associated with it.

Vladimir Nabokov

Scent is the most potent and bewitching substance in the gardener's repertory and yet it is the most neglected and least understood. The faintest waft is sometimes enough to induce feelings of hunger or anticipation, or to transport you back through time and space to a long-forgotten moment in your childhood. It can overwhelm you in an instant or simply tease you, creeping into your consciousness slowly and evaporating almost the moment it is detected. Each fragrance, whether sweet or spicy, light or heavy, comes upon you in its own way and evokes its own emotional response.

Stephen Lacey

 Seeing

Ken Wilbur makes an interesting distinction about seeing when he writes, "We can see with the eyes of the flesh or we can see with the eyes of the soul." But he is not the only one to see such a distinction. Paul Gauguin saw it when he said, "I shut my eyes in order to see." Oscar Wilde saw it when he wrote, "To look at a thing is very different from seeing a thing." George P. Marsh saw it when he said, "Sight is a faculty; seeing is an art." Margaret Prescott Montague called it seeing with the "inward eye"; e.e. cummings called it seeing with "the eyes of my eyes"; Jamake Highwater called it seeing "with your eyes at the edge of what is visible."

It is this kind of seeing that Teilhard de Chardin must be referring to when he wrote, "The whole life lies in the verb *seeing*"—that is, we see soul with our eyes if we see with the eye in our souls—and this makes what we see whole, and holy.

Looking for and enjoying beauty is another way to nourish the soul.
The universe is in the habit of making beauty. There are flowers and songs, snowflakes and smiles, acts of great courage, laughter between friends, a job well done, the smell of fresh-baked bread. Beauty is everywhere, ready to nourish the soul. It must only be seen to begin helping us.

Matthew Fox

As I experience it, appreciation of beauty is access to the soul. With beauty in our lives, we walk and carry ourselves more lightly and with a different look in our eyes. To look into the eyes of someone beholding beauty is to look through the windows of the soul. Anytime we catch a glimpse of soul, beauty is there; anytime we catch our breath and feel "How beautiful!," the soul is present.

Jean Shinoda Bolen

This visible world is wonderfully to be delighted in, and highly to be esteemed, because it is the theatre of God's righteous Kingdom.

Thomas Traherne

You must learn to look at the world twice. First you must bring your eyes together in front so you can see each droplet of rain on the grass, so you can see the smoke rising from an ant hill in the sunshine. Nothing should escape your notice. But you must learn to look again, with your eyes at the edge of what is visible. Now you must see dimly, if you wish to see things that are dim—visions, mist, and cloud people, animals which hurry past you in the dark. You must learn to look at the world twice if you wish to see all that there is to see.

Jamake Highwater

Learn to see, and then you'll know there is no end to the new worlds of our vision.

Carolos Castaneda

Look at everything as though you were seeing it either for the first or last time. Then your time on earth will be filled with glory.

Betty Smith

The greatest thing a human soul ever does in this world is to see something, and tell what it saw in a plain way. Hundreds of people can talk for one who can think, but thousands can think for one who can see. To see clearly is poetry, prophecy, and religion—all in one.

John Ruskin

The true mystery of the world is the visible, not the invisible.

Oscar Wilde

The real voyage of discovery consists of not in seeking
new landscapes but in having new eyes.

Marcel Proust

We are living in a world that is absolutely transparent and God is
shining through it all the time. God manifests Himself everywhere,
in everything—in people and in things and in nature and in events. . . .
The only thing is we don't see it. . . . I have no program for this seeing.
It is only given. But the gate of heaven is everywhere.

Thomas Merton

Look. This is your world! You can't not look. There is no other world.
This is your world; it is your feast. You inherited this; you inherited
these eyeballs; you inherited this world of color. Look at the greatness
of the whole thing. Look! Don't hesitate—look! Open your eyes.
Don't blink, and look, look—look further.

Chogyan Trungpa

Sounds

Joseph Campbell, in speaking of the role of sound in spirituality, notes
that rhythms "are conceived of as wings, wings of spiritual transport."
Whether it is the sound and rhythms of bells, chimes, chants, the re-
peating of sacred words or mantras, the beating of drums, the trickle of
water falling, or any of the myriad miracle tones of nature, "sound is one
of the most direct and simple means we have at our disposal for enchanting life and caring for the soul" (Thomas Moore). Andre Kostelanetz
recommends, "Everybody should have his personal sounds to listen for—
sounds that will make him exhilarated and alive or quiet and calm." On

the spiritual pathway, we should keep our ears open to discovering the sounds that still our souls or stimulate our spirits and tune our hearts toward them.

How wonderful, O Lord, are the works of your hands, the sun and the stars, the valleys and the hills, the rivers and lakes all disclose your presence. The beasts of the field, the birds of the air bespeak your wondrous will. In your goodness you have made us able to hear the music of the world, a divine voice sings through all creations.

Hebrew prayer

Sensitivity is beauty. If you sit quietly, or when you walk, listen to every sound. Let them all come in; hear their multiple beauty. Do it now. Sit quietly ... and hear what's going on about you. ... You heard that distant crow? The slapping of the rock with the wet cloth, the movement of the boy next to you, or the one away from you; the very far and the very near sounds. This listening cannot be learned from a book, or from anyone. It cultivates a quick, vivid sensitivity; listening sharpens the sense and the mind. Listen to every sound, let every sight come in, every sensation. Sensitivity is beauty, and to be sensitive you have to be done with likes and dislikes. I like this, I dislike that—sound, sight, feeling, idea, person. All come into consciousness and reveal themselves as they are. This is the sense of beauty. It is total and immediate.

Jiddu Krishnamurti

There is a Bodhisattva who attained enlightenment by concentrating insistently on every sound he heard, so Sakyamuni Buddha called him Kannon (Hearer of the cries of the world).

Bassui

The voice that beautifies the land!
The voice above,
The voice of thunder,
Among the dark clouds
Again and again it sounds,
The voice that beautifies the land.

The voice that beautifies the land!
The voice below,
The voice of the grasshopper,
Among the flowers and grasses
Again and again it sounds,
The voice that beautifies the land.

Navajo song

Your soul sometimes plays a note
Against the Sky's ear that excites
The birds and planets.

Stay close to any sounds
That make you glad you are alive.

Hafiz

The way to the heart is through the ears.

Katie Hurley

In our lives we can seek out experiences of sound that nourish the soul,
like a hike to a quiet spot in nature or to a stream or waterfall, or a visit
to a park that offers a retreat from city noise. The sounds of falling
water and blowing winds make real music that enters the soul and
gives it the aural nourishment it needs.

Thomas Moore

STATES OF BEING

The emotional frontier is truly the next frontier to conquer
in ourselves. The opportunity of this time is that we
can develop our emotional potential and accelerate
rather dramatically into a new state of being.

Doc Childre and Howard Martin

True spirituality is not a religion—it is a state of being.

Mary Hession

Being Attentive

There is a book called *Mindfulness in Plain English* by H. Gunaratana Maha-thera. In it, he gives a definition of mindfulness that I find powerful. "Mind-fulness is the English translation of the Pali word *Sati*. *Sati* is an activity. What exactly is that? . . . Mindfulness is mirror-thought. It reflects only what is presently happening and in exactly the way it is happening. There are no biases. Mindfulness is nonjudgmental observation. It is that ability of the mind to observe without criticism. With this ability, one sees things without condemnation or judgment. One is surprised by nothing. One simply takes a balanced interest in things exactly as they are in their natural states. One does not decide and does not judge. One just observes. . . . Mindfulness sees all experiences as equal, all thoughts as equal, all feel-ings as equal. Nothing is suppressed. Nothing is repressed. Mindfulness does not play favorites. Mindfulness is nonconceptual awareness." He ends by explaining, "Another English term for *Sati* is 'bare attention.'"

I love that translation—bare attention. How often in this world are we able to pay bare attention to something or someone without our minds splintering and scattering in twenty different directions? How often are we able to observe something or someone without bias, judgment, or criti-cism? Psychologist James Hillman calls attention "the cardinal psycho-logical virtue. On it depends perhaps the other cardinal virtues, for there can hardly be faith nor hope nor love for anything unless it first receives attention." Attention, *sati,* may be the cardinal spiritual virtue as well, and the best advice we may receive for connecting with our spiritual natures is as simple as, "Pay attention."

To pray is to pay attention to something or someone other than oneself. Whenever a man so concentrates his attention—on a landscape, a poem, a geometrical problem, an idol, or the True God—that he completely forgets his own ego and desires, he is praying.

W. H. Auden

The moment one gives close attention to any thing, even a blade of grass, it becomes a mysterious, awesome, indescribably magnificent world in itself.

Henry Miller

When we talk about understanding, surely it takes place only when the mind listens completely—the mind being your heart, your nerves, your ears—when you give your whole attention to it.

Jiddu Krishnamurti

The key to a Christian conception of studies is the realization that prayer consists of attention. It is the orientation of all the attention of which the soul is capable toward God. The quality of attention counts much in the quality of the prayer. Warmth of heart cannot make up for it.

Simone Weil

Do not undervalue attention. It means interest and also love. To know, to do, to discover, or to create you must give your heart to it—which means attention. All the blessings flow from it.

Nisargadatta Maharaj

Sometimes during the day, I consciously focus on some ordinary object and allow myself a momentary "paying attention." . . . What is called for is not intense concentration, with a knitting of the brows, but rather, the opposite, an awakening of the mind without fixing it anywhere, the quietness of pure attention. . . . What we may need to learn is that merely to look at things as they are, with bare attention, can be a religious act. We are thus enabled to comprehend God's creation as it is, our minds unclouded by egoistical emotions, and so made more aware of God himself.

Dom Aelred Graham

So having clearly understood the value of attention, wise men take pleasure in it, rejoicing in what the saints have practiced.

Buddha

A student once asked a Zen master to say something very philosophical and deep about Zen. The master said, "Attention." The student was disappointed and asked for something a bit more profound. The Zen master responded, "Attention, attention." That pretty much says it all. Any discipline that guides you to be more here and now, and helps you to sand off the encrusted layers of civilization, is a good method. Ultimately, you'll begin to expose the diamond within.

Emmett Miller

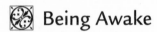 ## Being Awake

We are in a time so strange
that living equals dreaming,
and this teaches me that man
dreams his life, awake.

These lines are from a seventeenth-century play written by the Spaniard Calderón called *Life Is a Dream,* and they echo an Eastern idea that most of us go through the majority of our lives asleep, lost in the dream world of illusion, and that it is only the great sages and mystics who ever really awaken. In fact, twenty-five hundred years ago, after he had reached the state of enlightenment, Buddha was asked what he was, whether he was a god, a deva, or a saint, and he simply replied, "I am Awake."

Writes Malcolm Godwin, "The Hindu concept of *maya* clearly tells us that everything we appear to experience is actually an illusion, or a playful dream created by God. The original deity was supposedly either bored or lonely, so split itself into fragments which have forgotten who they are, and who play a sort of hide-and-seek with God in a universe of dreams." While the rest of us run around projecting our divinity onto others, crying, "Tag, you're it," the spiritually enlightened ones are those who are awakened to the fact that it's only a game and are able to stand still and say, "Tag, I'm it." Then, as the play says, we can dream our life, awake.

Awake, awake, great ones! The world is burning with misery. Can you sleep? Let us call and call till the sleeping gods awake, till the god within answers to the call. What more is in life? What greater work?

Swami Vivekananda

The spiritual life is, then, first of all a matter of keeping awake. We must not lose our sensitivity to spiritual inspiration.

Thomas Merton

Spirituality means waking up. Most people, even though they don't know it, are asleep. They're born asleep, they live asleep, they marry in their sleep, they breed children in their sleep, they die in their sleep without ever waking up. They never understand the loveliness and the beauty of this thing that we call human existence. You know—all mystics . . . are unanimous on one thing: that all is well, all is well. Though everything is a mess, all is well. Strange paradox, to be sure. But, tragically, most people never get to see that all is well because they are asleep. They are having a nightmare.

Anthony de Mello

Your vision will become clear only when you look into your heart. Who looks outside, dreams. Who looks inside, awakens.

Carl Jung

Holy Spirit,
Giving life to all life,
Moving all creatures,
Root of all things,
Washing them clean,
Wiping out their mistakes,
Healing their wounds,
You are our true life,
Luminous, wonderful,
Awakening the heart from its ancient sleep.

Hildegard von Bingen

Those who are awake live in a state of constant amazement.

Jack Kornfield

There is only one time when it is essential to awaken.
That time is now.

Buddha

The millions are awake enough for physical labor; but only one in a
million is awake enough for effective intellectual exertion, only one in
a hundred million to a poetic or divine life. To be awake is to be alive.

Henry David Thoreau

When the eternal knower, the rishi, wakes up in anyone, it proclaims,
"I must survive, I must create, I must be." That marks the moment
when human life truly begins.

Deepak Chopra

The breeze at dawn has secrets to tell you.
Don't go back to sleep.
You must ask for what you really want.
Don't go back to sleep.
People are going back and forth across the doorsill
Where the two worlds touch.
The door is round and open.
Don't go back to sleep.

Jalaluddin Rumi

Being Childlike

One morning on vacation with my family in Cancun, I went for a long walk on the tourist stretch of the beach. I walked for what seemed like several miles, and passed what seemed like hundreds of hotels, and saw what felt like thousands of people, but what I remember most is the children. Along that beach I passed American children and French children and Japanese children, I passed white children and brown children and black children, I passed United Nations of children, and every child that I passed, regardless of nationality, was doing one of two things: either running to and fro chasing the surf or digging in the sand with a bucket and a shovel of sorts. I was struck then, as I'm always struck now at any beach anywhere in my travels, with the universal simplicity and joy of children at play.

It is a universal religious and spiritual truth that children possess a wisdom that adults would do well to retain on their way to the kingdom of heaven. There is wisdom in being satisfied with sand and surf, with a bucket and a shovel. There is wisdom in wonder, in excitement, in living in the present moment, in letting emotions ebb and flow—all qualities of the child. Being in touch with our spiritual nature means being in touch with our childlike nature. Charles Baudelaire wrote, "Genius is childhood recaptured." So too could spirituality be called childhood recaptured.

Great sages have childlike natures. Before God they are always like children. They have no pride. Their strength is the strength of God, the strength of their Father. They have nothing to call their own. They are firmly convinced of that.

Ramakrishna

Picasso says it takes a long time to grow young, and I say it takes even longer to become as a little child. So that's the height we are striving for.

Myles Horton

People like you and I, though mortal of course like everyone else, do not grow old no matter how long we live. . . . [We] never cease to stand like curious children before the great mystery into which we were born.

Albert Einstein

If my heart can become pure and simple like that of a child, I think there probably can be no greater happiness than this.

Kitaro Nishida

To carry feelings of childhood into the powers of adulthood, to combine the child's sense of wonder and novelty with the appearances which every day for years has rendered familiar, this is the character and privilege of genius, and one of the marks which distinguish it from talent.

Samuel Taylor Coleridge

The great man is he who does not lose his childlike heart.

Mencius

Jesus called a child over, placed it in their midst, and said, "Amen, I say unto you, unless you turn and become like a little child, you will not enter the kingdom of heaven. Whoever humbles himself like this child is the greatest in the kingdom of heaven."

Matthew 18:2–4

It is our Child who knows the reality of the world of dreams, imagination, and visions.

Anne Brennan

Grown men can learn from very little children for the hearts of little children are pure. Therefore, the Great Spirit may show to them many things which older people miss.

Black Elk

Your religion is one which challenges the ordinary human standards by holding that the ideal of life is the spirit of a little child. We tend to glorify adulthood and wisdom and worldly prudence, but the Gospel reverses all this. The Gospel says that the inescapable condition of entrance into the divine fellowship is that we turn and become as a little child. As against our natural judgment we must become tender and full of wonder and unspoiled by the hard skepticism on which we so often pride ourselves. But when we really look into the heart of a child, willful as he or she may be, we are often ashamed. God has sent children into the world, not only to replenish it, but to serve as sacred reminders of something ineffably precious which we are always in danger of losing. The sacrament of childhood is thus a continuing revelation.

Elton Trueblood

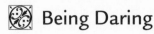 Being Daring

Ask yourself for one moment what your feelings have been on the eve of some act involving courage, whether it be physical courage, or moral or intellectual . . . what has happened to you? If it has really called forth courage, has it not felt something like this: "I cannot do this. This is too much for me. I shall ruin myself if I take this risk. I cannot take the leap, it's impossible. All of me will be gone if I do this, and I cling to myself." And then supposing the Spirit has conquered and you have done this impossible thing, do you find afterward that you possess yourself in a sense that you never had before? That there is more of you?

J. N. Figgis put into perfect words my experience of skydiving. The night before, I was afraid, afraid I would let myself and my friends down by failing to make the leap, by failing to have the necessary courage to make true this dream. The fear dogged me the next day, but in spite of that, or maybe because of it, I have never felt so alive, so on the edge of living. And after the jump, it was true that there was more of me somehow, that my spirit had expanded both through experiencing my own courage and faith and through the reward of feeling what it's like, just for a brief moment in time, to soar like the birds on the wings of spirit.

Living at risk is jumping off the cliff and building
your wings on the way down.

Ray Bradbury

I will not die an unlived life. I will not live in fear of falling or catching
fire. I choose to inhabit my days, to allow my living to open me, to make
me less afraid, more accessible, to loosen my heart until it becomes a
wing, a torch, a promise. I choose to risk my significance; to live so that
which comes to me as seed goes to the next as blossom and that which
comes to me as blossom, goes on as fruit.

Dawna Markova

Life ought to be a struggle of desire toward adventures
whose nobility will fertilize the soul.

Rebecca West

For without risk there is no faith, and the greater the risk,
the greater the faith.

Søren Kierkegaard

Those who are afraid to make mistakes serve a god of fear.
Their love is incomplete. Go forth boldly. Have the courage
to live your vision in spite of your fears.

Ken Carey

Attempt something so impossible that unless God is in it,
it's doomed to failure.

John Haggai

Does not the history of the world show that there would have
been no romance in life if there had been no risks?

Gandhi

One has to abandon altogether the search for security, and reach out to
the risk of living with both arms. One has to embrace the world like a
lover. One has to accept pain as a condition of existence. One has to
court doubt and darkness as the cost of knowing. One needs a will
stubborn in conflict, but apt always to total acceptance of every
consequence of living and dying.

Morris L. West

The universe will reward you for taking risks on its behalf.

Shakti Gawain

Risks must be taken because the greatest hazard in life is to risk
nothing. The person who risks nothing does nothing, has nothing,
and becomes nothing. He may avoid suffering and sorrow, but he
simply cannot learn and feel and change and grow and love and live.
Chained by his certitudes, he is a slave, he's forfeited his freedom.
Only the person who risks is truly free.

Leo Buscaglia

 Being Grateful

One of the wisest things I've ever read is by Richard Baker-Roshi, who
wrote, "All we have in life is what we notice." Really, if you think about it,
it's true. For example, if you're walking down the street and you notice
twenty dollars on the sidewalk and no one in sight, you'll pick it up and
put it in your pocket and be really happy. Sure, the twenty bucks made
you happy, but what *really* made you happy was noticing the twenty bucks,
because if you walked down the sidewalk and *didn't* notice it, you'd have
no reason to be happy, even though the twenty was still there! So the logic
goes, if all we notice in life is what's wrong, we will have a life filled with
wrong things; if all we notice in life is what's ugly, we'll have a life filled with
ugly things. Our emotions and experiences are driven by what we notice;
therefore, one of the best ways to have satisfying emotions and more
fulfilling experiences is to notice more of what satisfies and fulfills us.

This is the power of the practice of gratitude, the power that leads
Meister Eckhart to contend, "If the only prayer you ever say in your entire
life is thank you, it will be enough." When we practice gratitude, we train
ourselves to notice what we have to be thankful for, and the more we

notice what we have to be thankful for, more of what we have to be thankful for comes into our lives. It is circular reasoning for sure, but it is wise in its purity and simplicity. Saying prayers of thanks or meditating with thanksgiving is one of the surest ways to increase our sense of being blessed by spirit.

Let us rise up and be thankful,
for if we didn't learn a lot today, at least we learned a little,
and if we didn't learn a little,
at least we didn't get sick,
and if we got sick, at least we didn't die;
so, let us all be thankful.

Buddha

Gratitude unlocks the fullness of life. It turns what we have into enough, and more. It turns denial into acceptance, chaos to order, confusion to clarity. It can turn a meal into a feast, a house into a home, a stranger into a friend. Gratitude makes sense of our past, brings peace for today, and creates a vision for tomorrow.

Melody Beattie

To speak gratitude is courteous and pleasant, to enact gratitude is generous and noble, but to live gratitude is to touch Heaven.

Johannes A. Gaertner

Gratitude is our most direct line to God and the angels. If we take the time, no matter how crazy and troubled we feel, we can find something to be thankful for. The more we seek gratitude, the more reason the angels will give us for gratitude and joy to exist in our lives.

Terry Lynn Taylor

Gratitude is the sign of noble souls.

Aesop

God has two dwellings; one in heaven, and the other
in a meek and thankful heart.

Izaak Walton

You simply will not be the same person two months from now after
consciously giving thanks each day for the abundance that exists in
your life. And you will have set in motion an ancient spiritual law:
the more you have and are grateful for, the more will be given you.

Sarah Ban Breathnach

When you arise in the morning, give
thanks for the morning light.
Give thanks for your life and your strength.
Give thanks for your food
and give thanks for the joy of living.
And if you see no reason for giving thanks,
rest assured that the fault is in yourself.

Chief Tecumseh

 Being Inspired

In Plato's myth of Er from the *Republic,* he teaches that when souls are
about to incarnate, they are given a guide called a *daimon,* or in Roman
terms, a *genius.* This spiritual companion follows you into the world, and
when you lose your way or forget who you are, he or she guides you back
to your true self and leads you onward toward your destiny.

This spiritual companion, what some might call a guardian angel, is the source of inspiration as well. It is the voice that whispers in your ear; it is the thought that burns in your brain; it is the fire that sears your soul; it is the idea or the image or the desire that will not let you go. To be inspired means to be open to what poet William Stafford calls "following the little god who speaks only to me." To be inspired means being attentive to what Publius Ovidius Naso called the "deity within us who breathes that divine fire by which we are animated." We should ask ourselves, "What inspires me?" but we should also ask ourselves, "*Who* inspires me?" because the answer will lead us to the divine spirit who in turn will lead us to our destiny.

Straight-away the ideas flow in upon me, directly from God, and not only do I see distinct themes in my mind's eye, but they are clothed in the right forms, harmonies, and orchestration.

Johannes Brahms

Far away in the sunshine are my highest inspirations. I may not reach them, but I can look up and see the beauty, believe in them and try to follow where they lead.

Louisa May Alcott

It may seem a little old-fashioned, always to begin one's work with prayer, but I never undertake a hymn without first asking the good Lord to be my inspiration.

Fanny Crosby

Who knows where inspiration comes from? Perhaps it arises from desperation. Perhaps it comes from the flukes of the universe, the kindness of the muses.

Amy Tan

Inspiration is a fragile thing . . . just a breeze, touching the green foliage of a city park, just a whisper from the soul of a friend. Just a line of verse clipped from some book. Inspiration . . . who can say where it is born, and why it leaves us? Who can tell the reasons for its being or not being? Only this . . . I can think. Inspiration comes from the Heart of Heaven to give the lift of wings, and the breath of divine music to those of us who are earthbound.

Margaret Sangster

Perpetual inspiration is as necessary to the life of goodness, holiness, and happiness as perpetual respiration is necessary to animal life.

Andrew Bonar Law

I have inspiration and feelings of being alive most every day I live. I call them part of the joy of living, and they are there for all of us.

Judy Collins

There never was a great soul that did not have some divine inspiration.

Marcus T. Cicero

Inspiration demands that active cooperation of the intellect joined with enthusiasm, and it is under such conditions that marvelous conceptions, with all that is excellent and divine, come into being.

Giorgio Vasari

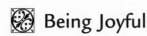 Being Joyful

The power and mystery of a concept is often revealed in the dictionary by the sheer number of other words it takes to capture its meaning. Thus is the case with *joy,* which the dictionary dances around and drapes with such words as "to rejoice; to be glad; to delight; to exult; to feel intense and especially ecstatic or exultant happiness; to feel elation and rapture and bliss." I like the definition from the Buddhist holy book the Dhammapada: "Let us live joyfully. Let us live on spiritual bliss, radiating spiritual light."

Rebbe Nachman admonishes us, "Always remember, joy is not incidental to spiritual quest. It is vital." How vitally we would live if we lived on spiritual bliss, radiating spiritual light. With this vitality we would become one with the world, for as Martin Buber describes it, "at the beating heart of the universe is holy joy."

> Joy is the holy fire that keeps our purpose warm
> and our intelligence aglow.
>
> Helen Keller

> While with an eye made quiet by the power of harmony,
> and the deep power of joy,
> We see into the life of things.
>
> William Wordsworth

> One filled with joy preaches without preaching.
>
> Mother Teresa

> Joy in the universe, and keen curiosity about it all—
> that has been my religion.
>
> John Burroughs

If the sight of the blue skies fills you with joy, if a blade of grass springing up in the fields has power to move you, if the simple things of nature have a message that you understand, rejoice, for your soul is alive.

Eleonora Duse

Eternal joy is the end of the ways of God. The message of all religions is that the Kingdom of God is peace and joy. And it is the message of Christianity. But eternal joy is not to be reached by living on the surface. It is rather attained by breaking through the surface, by penetrating the deep things of ourselves, of our world, and of God. The moment in which we reach the last depth of our lives is the moment in which we can experience the joy that has eternity within it, the hope that cannot be destroyed, and the truth on which life and death are built. For in the depth is truth; and in the depth is hope; and in the depth is joy.

Paul Tillich

Joy is a constituent of life, a necessity of life; it is an element of life's value and life's power. As every person has need of joy, so too, every person has a right to joy. . . . It is a condition of religious living.

Paul Wilhelm von Keppler

As long as there have been human beings, they have felt too little joy; that alone, my brothers and sisters, is our original sin.

Friedrich Nietzsche

If the day and the night are such that you greet them with joy, and life emits a fragrance like flowers and sweet-scented herbs, is more elastic, more starry, more immortal—that is your success. All nature is your congratulation, and you have cause momentarily to bless yourself.

Henry David Thoreau

Religion without joy—it is no religion.

Theodore Parker

How necessary it is to cultivate a spirit of joy. It is a psychological truth that the physical acts of reverence and devotion make one feel devout. The courteous gesture increases one's respect for others. To act lovingly is to begin to feel loving, and certainly to act joyfully brings joy to others which in turn makes one feel joyful. I believe we are called to the duty of delight.

Dorothy Day

Ancient Egyptians believed that upon death they would be asked two questions and their answers would determine whether they could continue their journey in the afterlife. The first question was, "Did you bring joy?" The second was, "Did you find joy?"

Leo Buscaglia

Being on Purpose

Once, sitting with my little family in a little church in a little town on a little morning known as Christmas, I heard a minister say a little something that has stayed with me to this day. "When God wants something done on Earth," he told us, "a child is born." I had heard this idea many times in my life, that we are all born with a God-given purpose and it is up to us to discover it, but I had never heard it stated so simply, so eloquently, and so powerfully.

As beautiful as that statement is, however, I don't think we have to believe that it is true. We can be spiritual and believe that we define our own purpose, that it is up to us to infuse our lives with meaning and then live in accordance with that meaning. In other words, instead of discovering our purpose, we can create it; instead of being used for a purpose, we can purposefully use ourselves. Perhaps it matters less to live the spiritual life where we think purpose comes from and how it is divined than it matters that we simply live our lives with the sense of being on purpose.

You know when you were little that you were born for something special and no matter what happened to you, that couldn't be erased. . . . Sorry to tell you, but you had it right years ago, and then you forgot. You were born with a mystical purpose.

Marianne Williamson

Everything on the earth has a purpose, every disease an herb to cure it, and every person a mission.

Mourning Dove

You can come to understand your purpose in life by slowing down and feeling your heart's desires.

Marcia Wieder

When you are inspired by some great purpose, some extraordinary project, all your thoughts break their bounds: your mind transcends limitations, your consciousness expands in every direction, and you find yourself in a new, great, and wonderful world. Dormant forces, faculties, and talents become alive, and you discover yourself to be a greater person by far than you ever dreamed yourself to be.

Patanjali

The purpose of a man's heart are deep waters, but a man of understanding draws them out.

Proverbs 20:5

We are not powerless specks of dust drifting around in the wind, blown by random destiny. We are, each of us, like beautiful snowflakes—unique, and born for a specific reason and purpose.

Elisabeth Kübler-Ross

Every moment comes to you pregnant with divine purpose. . . . Once it leaves your hands and your power to do with it as you please, it plunges into eternity, to remain forever what you made it.

Fulton J. Sheen

Nothing contributes so much to tranquilize the mind as a steady purpose—a point on which the soul may fix its intellectual eye.

Mary Wollstonecraft Shelley

To me the sole hope of human salvation lies in teaching Man to regard himself as an experiment in the realization of God, to regard his hands as God's hand, his brain as God's brain, his purpose as God's purpose.

George Bernard Shaw

What we need are mental and spiritual giants who are aflame with a purpose. . . . We're a race ready for crusade, for we've recognized that we're a race on this continent that can work out its own salvation.

Nannie Burroughs

 Being Present

In Ram Dass's 1970s spiritual classic *Be Here Now,* his third chapter is called "Cookbook for a Sacred Life." If there could be such a thing as a recipe for sacred living, surely being present would be a main ingredient.

However, it's not an easy ingredient to procure! The past and the future vie for shelf space and often obscure our clear view of the present. How often are we still digesting meals from the past, or planning menus for the future?

Several years ago I was visiting New York when I kept noticing the words NO DAY BUT TODAY written on the top of many of the taxi cabs. Not understanding the context at the time (it was the name of a song from the Broadway musical *Rent*), it felt very surreal to see all these cabs passing by reminding me of the wisdom of being present, but let me tell you, it worked! To return to the cooking analogy, how many times have we gone to the grocery store to pick up one ingredient only to find we've returned home with ten while forgetting the one thing we went there for? Maybe we need to carry around a yellow Post-It note (or be carried around by a yellow cab) with the words NO DAY BUT TODAY on it to remind us of the necessary ingredient of being present to cooking up a sacred life.

There is no place where the Presence of God is not, only people who are not fully present in the places where they are. You have only to be present to know all you need to know.

Ken Carey

Be attentive to time and how you spend it. Nothing is more precious. This is evident when you recall that in one tiny moment heaven may be gained or lost. God, the master of time, never gives the future. He gives only the present, moment by moment.

The Cloud of Unknowing

We inhabit ourselves without valuing ourselves, unable to see that here, now, this very moment is sacred; but once it's gone— its value is incontestable.

Joyce Carol Oates

Only when your consciousness is totally focused on the moment you are in can you receive whatever gift, lesson, or delight that moment has to offer.

Barbara De Angelis

The present moment is a powerful goddess.

Johann Wolfgang von Goethe

Yesterday is ashes, tomorrow wood.
Only today does the fire burn brightly.

Eskimo proverb

The present contains all that there is. It is holy ground;
for it is the past, and it is the future.

Alfred North Whitehead

What we are talking about is learning to live in the present moment, in the now. When you aren't distracted by your own negative thinking, when you don't allow yourself to get lost in moments that are gone or yet to come, you are left with this moment. This moment—now—truly is the only moment you have. It is beautiful and special. Life is simply a series of such moments to be experienced one right after another. If you attend to the moment you are in and stay connected to your soul and remain happy, you will find that your heart is filled with positive feelings.

Sydney Banks

When you live completely today there is a great intensity
in it and in its beauty.

Krishna

Do we need to make a special effort to enjoy the beauty of the blue sky?
Do we have to practice to be able to enjoy it? No, we just enjoy it. Each
second, each minute of our lives can be like this. Wherever we are, any
time, we have the capacity to enjoy the sunshine, the presence of each
other, even the sensation of our breathing. We don't need to go to
China to enjoy the blue sky. We don't have to travel into the future to
enjoy our breathing. We can be in touch with these things right now.

Thich Nhat Hanh

What we are left with then is the present, the only time where miracles
happen. We place the past and the future as well into the hands of
God. The biblical statement that "time shall be no more" means
that we will one day live fully in the present, without obsessing
about past or future.

Marianne Williamson

 Being Reverent

Reverence is a feeling or attitude of deep respect, love, and awe, especially
for something sacred. It is the feeling that causes us to drop to our knees
in worship; it is the feeling that causes us to raise our voices in praise.

Once, on the island of Santorini, I wandered into a store along the
tourist area where an older Greek man sold Greek Orthodox icons, mostly
religious scenes and figures painted onto pieces of wood. His face was
beautiful: worn, deeply creased, thick-jowled, and gruff, but full of light
and love and kindness nonetheless. The icons were hanging on the wall,

and each time I would ask to see one, he would take it off the wall, tenderly kiss the face of it, offer it to me like he was offering me the most precious of jewels, and when I was finished looking at it, enthusiastically kiss it again before returning it to the wall. I asked him about some of the Greek writing on the icons, and what the symbols meant. He answered in broken English that I couldn't really understand, but still I kept asking, because I was captivated not by his *meaning* but by his *manner* of explaining. He was in love with those icons as he was in love with his religion; the way he talked about them was no different than how a young man would talk about a beautiful woman he had just met and fallen irreversibly in love with—tirelessly, ecstatically, with an equal mix of respect and awe.

He was also a good salesman. I bought two icons and was sold an invaluable lesson on reverence.

Reverence is that altered state of consciousness when you feel awe and wonder because you know you are in the presence of Spirit. Reverence enwraps you in perfect peace because there is no past or future, only the present moment, and you are one with Heaven and earth. There is no distinction between body and soul.

Sarah Ban Breathnach

The soul of the Christian religion is reverence.

Johann Wolfgang von Goethe

Reverence is a perception of the soul. Only the personality can perceive Life without reverence. Reverence is a natural aspect of authentic empowerment because the soul reveres all of life.

Gary Zukav

Because
There is nothing
Outside of my Master's body

I try
To show reverence
To all things.

Hafiz

What we call love is in its essence reverence for life.

Albert Schweitzer

Long ago there was a mighty king who lived a sheltered and indulgent life inside the walls of his castle. One day he decided to venture into his kingdom to see what he might experience and learn. He soon came upon a monk, and in a voice accustomed to instant obedience, he said, "Monk, teach me about heaven and hell!" The monk looked up at the mighty king and in an annoyed voice said, "I can't teach you about heaven and hell. You're too stupid. You're just an indulgent slob. The teachings I have are for pure and holy people. You don't even come close. Get out of my way!"

The king became furious. He was appalled that this monk dared to speak to him in this manner. In a fit of rage, he pulled out his sword to chop off the monk's head.

"That's hell," said the monk confidently.

The king was stunned. He realized that this courageous monk had risked his life to teach him this lesson about hell. In deep gratitude and humility, the king put down his sword and bowed reverently to the monk.

"And that's heaven," said the monk softly.

Jonathan Robinson

The first condition of human goodness is something to love;
the second, something to revere.

George Eliot

When my life opens up very clearly, I can't help, from the depths of my
heart, wanting to bow. When the mind that wants to bow to enemies
and friends and demons and gods and evils and Buddhas and good
friends and bad people—when this feeling comes tumbling out of my
deep life, then I am already master of the whole world, I control the
entire world. I become friends with all humans and other beings.

Hara Akegarasu

 Being Silent

I left my home in California one summer to go on a driving tour of some
of the most sacred sites in the Southwest, seeking a deeper relationship
with my own spirituality through the spirituality of place. Everywhere I
went—the Grand Canyon, Sedona, Monument Valley, Canyon de Chelly,
Chimayó—there was one common thread running through the spiritual
experience I sought.

People would not shut up.

When I got back home, I met up for dinner with my best friend, Shannan,
to tell her about my trip. "So," she asked, "did you work on the book you
had planned?"

"No, I got a new idea for a book while I was gone," I told her, lips con-
torting in faintly disguised disgust. "It's going to be called *America, Shut
the Hell Up.*"

Not a very spiritual response, I'll admit. But it wasn't as if people were
talking about the magic of the place or the spirit dwelling within or
sharing their heartfelt responses. Most conversations that intruded upon

my consciousness were about the most mundane things, empty words polluting the air. One case in point: the man who, while walking down an ancient ladder into a more ancient Native American kiva where even more ancient Native American spiritual rituals were held, was telling his companion about the great deal he had gotten on his Nikes at the outlet store.

A fractured rainbow
Is straining under thunder clouds with
Cathedral quiet.

"Cathedral quiet," James Kirkup wrote, and in that simple pairing of words, he illustrates that there is something religious about silence. "Would you talk this much if you were in a church?" I wanted to ask them. And then, "And when are you not in a church?"

I could write a book.

If you ask us, "What is silence?" we will answer, "It is the Great Mystery. The holy silence is God's voice."

Ohiyesa

In the attitude of silence the soul finds the path in a clearer light, and what is elusive and deceptive resolves itself into crystal clearness.

Gandhi

Silence is not an absence of sound but rather a shifting of attention toward sounds that speak to the soul. In a moment of silence you may feel your heartbeat or hear your breathing. Silence is a positive kind of hearing, which requires turning off the knob that tunes in to active, literal life and tuning on the one that amplifies the movements of the soul.

Thomas Moore

God's one and only voice is silence.

Herman Melville

There is something greater and purer than what the mouth utters.
Silence illuminates our souls,
whispers to our hearts,
and brings them together.

Kahlil Gibran

Through the orifice of silence,
the whole geyser of Bliss,
perpetually shoots up and flows over the soul.

Paramahansa Yogananda

God is the friend of silence. See how nature—trees, flowers, grass—
grows in silence; see the stars, the moon, and the sun, how they move
in silence. . . . We need silence to be able to touch souls.

Mother Teresa

Not only a truer knowledge,
but a greater power comes to one
in the quietude and silence of a mind
that, instead of bubbling on the surface,
can go to its own depths and listen.

Sri Aurobindo

The holy time is quiet as a nun
Breathless with adoration.

William Wordsworth

To find God there must be calm within, certain senses must be hushed. Tossed around as we are, if God wishes to speak to us, his voice, small and still, will be lost in the hubbub of our daily lives; the rackets and noise drowning our minds will prevent his penetration into that seclusion we call "heart"—the living witness of that life in us which is most sacred and most true; the life we call inner and spiritual.

J. M. Dechanet

Let us be silent that we may hear the whispers of the gods.

Ralph Waldo Emerson

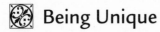 # Being Unique

God picks up the reed-flute world and blows.
Each note is a need coming through one of us,
a passion, a longing-pain.
Remember the lips
where the wind-breath originated,
and let your note be clear.
Don't try to end it.
Be your note.

Rumi

The original definition of *spirit* is "breath, or to breathe." When we are in touch with spirit, we are in touch with the Divine that blows breath through us and makes music. We don't try to block the music, or change the note; we simply allow it to come through. As Rumi teaches, to be in touch with spirit, we must be our own unique self; we must be *our* note.

The privilege of a lifetime is being who you are.

Joseph Campbell

You must not let your life run in the ordinary way; do something that nobody else has done, something that will dazzle the world. Show that God's creative principle works in you.

Paramahansa Yogananda

Nature never repeats herself and the possibilities of one human soul will never be found in another.

Elizabeth Cady Stanton

There is a vitality, a life-force, a quickening that is translated through you into action, and because there is only one of you in all time, this expression is unique. And if you block it, it will never exist through any other medium and it will be lost—the world will not have it. It is not your business to determine how good it is, nor how valuable it is, nor how it compares with other expressions. It is your business to keep it yours, clearly and directly, to keep the channel open.

Martha Graham

Millions of men have lived to fight, build palaces and boundaries, shape destinies and societies; but the compelling force of all times has been the force of originality and creation profoundly affecting the roots of human spirit.

Ansel Adams

There may be intelligences or sparks of the divinity in millions—but they are not Souls till they acquire identities, till each one is personally itself. . . . As various as the Lives of Men are—so various become their souls, and thus does God make individual beings, Souls, Identical Souls of the sparks of his own essence.

John Keats

You can see the beauty of Christ in each individual person, in that which is most his, most human, most personal to him, in things which an ascetic might advise you sternly to get rid of.

Thomas Merton

Everyone is unique. Compare not yourself with anyone else lest you spoil God's curriculum.

Baal Shem Tov

The snow-goose need not bathe to make itself white. Neither should you do anything but be yourself.

Lao Tzu

It is only to the individual that a soul is given.

Albert Einstein

VALUES

Your soul has a single basic function—
the act of valuing.

Ayn Rand

If we are to go forward, we must go back and
rediscover those precious values:
that all reality hinges on moral foundations
and that all reality has spiritual control.

Martin Luther King, Jr.

 Charity

We have narrowed down how we see charity in this culture, viewing it primarily as giving to the poor or needy, as something material we donate that provides us with a tax write-off. But this is only one definition of charity, and by reducing it in this way, we destroy its spiritual richness. A better definition of charity comes from the dictionary: "giving voluntarily to those in need; almsgiving; an institution or organization for helping those in need; a kindness, benevolence; tolerance in judging others; love of one's fellow human beings." Charity is also compassion, service, sympathy, and concern for others. Charity is love painted in broad strokes, reaching out to others we may never see or come to know simply out of the breadth of our spirits. Mohammed tells his followers, "Charity is incumbent on each person every day. Charity is assisting anyone, moving and carrying their wares, saying a good word. Every step one takes walking to prayer is charity. Showing the way is charity." Though there's no tax write-off for the charitable contribution of a smile, of a caring touch, of a kind word, of the gift of time or attention, of tolerance for another's shortcomings, this too is charity, and it is incumbent upon anyone wishing to further themselves on the spiritual road to do so through the vehicle of charity.

The desire for power in excess caused angels to fall; the desire for knowledge in excess caused man to fall; but in charity is no excess, neither can man or angels come in danger by it.

Francis Bacon

Charity never humiliated him who profited from it, nor ever bound him by the chains of gratitude, since it was not to him but to God that the gift was made.

Antoine de Saint-Exupéry

To pity distress is but human; to relieve it is Godlike.

Horace Mann

Charity. To love human beings insofar as they are nothing.
That is to love them as God does.

Simone Weil

Did universal charity prevail, earth would be a heaven, and hell a fable.

Charles Caleb Colton

There is no real religious experience that does not express itself in charity.

C. H. Dodd

Though Christian charity sounds a very cold thing to people whose
heads are full of sentimentality, and though it is quite distinct from
affection, yet it leads to affection. The difference between a Christian
and a worldly person is not that the worldly person has only affections
or "likings" and the Christian has only "charity." The worldly person
treats certain people kindly because he or she "likes" them: the
Christian, trying to treat everyone kindly, finds him or herself liking
more and more people as they go on—including people they could
not even have imagined themselves liking at the beginning.

C. S. Lewis

We are obligated to be more scrupulous in fulfilling the
commandment of charity than any other positive commandment
because charity is the sign of a righteous man.

Maimonides

Prayer carries us half way to God, fasting brings us to the door
of His palace, and alms-giving procures us admission.

the Koran

Every good act is charity. A man's true wealth hereafter is the good
that he does in this world to his fellows.

Mohammed

 # Compassion

Joseph Campbell, best known for his work in illuminating the archetypal
elements of the hero's journey, says, "The purpose of the journey is compassion. When you have come past all the pairs of opposites you have
reached compassion."

I like thinking of compassion in that way, as present when we have
transcended all opposites. It reminds me of something Mayumi Oda said,
that "compassion is really the understanding of the whole world as one,
that there's no separation between me and you." It's different from sympathy, because when sympathy is present, there is *me* feeling sorry for *your*
sorrow, two spirits separated by individual circumstances. When true
compassion is present, there is only *us* feeling *our* sorrow, one spirit joined
by universal circumstances. It follows that one of our purest expressions
of spirituality will be compassion, both the means and the end of the
heroic journey.

When we feel compassion, we take the shape of that which we see, we
understand a thing; we take its form, feel its weight, see its color, hear
its sound, know its mind, grow within its heart. We think as poets,
and understand as angels.

Karen Goldman

You may call God love, you may call God goodness.
But the best name for God is compassion.

Meister Eckhart

Man is never nearer the Divine than in his compassionate moments.

Joseph H. Hertz

The whole idea of compassion is based on a keen awareness of the
interdependence of all these living beings, which are all part of
one another, and all involved in one another.

Thomas Merton

Compassion is not sentiment but is making justice and doing works
of mercy. Compassion is not a moral commandment but a flow and
overflow of the fullest human and divine energies.

Matthew Fox

The wise man learns what draws God
Near.

It is the beauty of compassion
In your heart.

Hafiz

If you want others to be happy,
practice compassion.
If you want to be happy,
practice compassion.

the Dalai Lama

A human being is a part of the whole called by us universe, a part limited in time and space. He experiences himself, his thoughts and feeling as something separated from the rest, a kind of optical delusion of his consciousness. This delusion is a kind of prison for us, restricting us to our personal desires and to affection for a few persons nearest to us. Our task must be to free ourselves from this prison by widening our circle of compassion to embrace all living creatures and the whole of nature in its beauty.

Albert Einstein

When your mind is liberated, your heart floods with compassion.

Thich Nhat Hanh

Every praying Christian, every person who has an encounter with God, must have a passionate concern for his or her brother and sister, his or her neighbor. To treat any of these as if he were less than the child of God is to deny the validity of one's spiritual existence.

Bishop Desmond Tutu

 Faith

On the recommendation of Debbie, one of my closest soul friends, I've just begun Rosemary Mahoney's *The Singular Pilgrim*. In the introduction, Mahoney writes of a pilgrimage where each August 15, the Feast of the Assumption, the Greek Orthodox faithful travel great distances to pay homage to an icon of the Virgin housed in a church on a hill on the tiny island of Tinos. The pilgrims arrive by ferry, and the moment the boat touches the dock, they "rush forward, fall to the ground, and begin making their way to the church on hands and knees," some even slithering the half-mile on their bellies, praying for miracles and mercy. By the time they arrive, several hours of crawling later, she writes that "their hands and knees are galled into raw and bloody emblems of their belief. Once before the icon they prostrate themselves in a rapture of spiritual desire." Mahoney writes of herself, "I am attached to reason and am not easily awed by the miraculous powers of the Virgin Mary, but I was awed by her pilgrims. It wasn't their religion that interested me so much as their faith, the palpable surge of soul."

I stopped and underlined that sentence, intrigued by the distinction between religion and faith. Where I once thought they went hand in hand, it now occurs to me that they can also be divergent, that some people, having lost their faith, turn to religion, and other people shed their religion when they find faith. I realized that I, too, am less interested in religion than I am in faith, "that palpable surge of soul." For all of us pilgrims, faith accompanies us on our spiritual journey, and at the same time, we acquire more faith as we journey.

Faith is an excitement and an enthusiasm: it is a condition of intellectual magnificence to which we must cling as to a treasure, and not squander on our way through life.

George Sand

Faith is deliberate confidence in the character of God whose ways you may not understand at the time.

Oswald Chambers

It is the heart which perceives God and not the reason. That is what faith is: God perceived by the heart, not by the reason.

Blaise Pascal

Faith is the soul's adventure.

William Bridges

I have one life and one chance to make it count for something. . . .
I'm free to choose what that something is, and the something I've
chosen is my faith. Now, my faith goes beyond theology and religion
and requires considerable work and effort. My faith demands—this is
not optional—my faith demands that I do whatever I can, wherever
I am, whenever I can, for as long as I can with whatever I have to
try to make a difference.

Jimmy Carter

I feel no need for any other faith than my faith in the kindness of
human beings. I am so absorbed in the wonder of earth and the life
upon it that I cannot think of heaven and angels.

Pearl S. Buck

Faith ought not to be a puny thing. If we believe,
we should believe like giants.

Mary McLeod Bethune

Faith is spiritualized imagination.

Henry Ward Beecher

Faith is the response of our spirits to beckonings of the eternal.

George A. Buttrick

Faith is the centerpiece of a connected life. It allows us to live by the
grace of invisible strands. It is a belief in a wisdom superior to our own.
Faith becomes a teacher in the absence of fact.

Terry Tempest Williams

God has not called me to be successful; he has called me to be faithful.

Mother Teresa

I maintain that faith is a pathless land,
and you can approach it by any path whatsoever,
by any religion, by any sect.

Jiddhu Krishnamurti

 # Forgiveness

Science is starting to catch on to what the world's religious and spiritual traditions have always known: there is tremendous power in forgiveness. Studies on forgiveness date back only ten years, but recently there has been an explosion of interest on the subject, with research projects appearing left and right exploring every aspect of forgiveness, including the benefits to our physical health, the health of our relationships, the health of our cultures, and the health of our psyches. While it seems rather obvious that forgiveness is beneficial, what is far less obvious is just exactly how to go about forgiving. Researchers are starting to explore this enigma as well, examining, among other techniques, how spiritual practices like meditation and prayer increase our ability to forgive. They are also studying forgiveness as both cause and effect, looking at how being religious or spiritual might increase our ability to forgive, as well as how being able to forgive might increase our experience of religion or spirituality.

We don't have to wait until the research is in to incorporate forgiveness as part of our spiritual practice, to allow our spirituality to make us more forgiving, and to allow our experiences of forgiveness to make us more spiritual.

Forgive, forgive, and forgive some more; never stop forgiving, for the temptation to project and judge will always be there as long as you are living in the body. Forgiveness is the key to peace and happiness, and gives us everything that we could possibly want.

Gerald G. Jampolsky

To err is human, to forgive, divine.

Alexander Pope

What could you want forgiveness cannot give? Do you want peace?
Forgiveness offers it. Do you want happiness, a quiet mind, a certainty
of purpose, and a sense of worth and beauty that transcends the world?
Do you want care and safety, and the warmth of sure protection
always? Do you want a quietness that cannot be disturbed, a gentleness
that never can be hurt, a deep abiding comfort, and a rest so perfect it
can never be upset? All this forgiveness offers you.

A Course in Miracles

Where there is forgiveness, there is God Himself.

The Adi Granth

When Jesus was crucified, Roman soldiers pierced him. And Jesus
prayed for his enemies: "Father, forgive them; for they know not what
they do." Even at the moment of death on the cross, Jesus was so
earnest in forgiving. His very last act was motivated by his love for his
enemies. He was the supreme form of giving—a paragon of love. The
example of Jesus Christ is the absolute standard for all mankind. Just
imagine an entire nation composed of Jesus-like men. What would you
call it? The Kingdom of Heaven on earth—it could be nothing less.

Sun Myung Moon

He that cannot forgive others, breaks the bridge over which he
himself must pass if he would ever reach heaven; for everyone
has need to be forgiven.

George Herbert

We must be saved by the final form of love which is forgiveness.

Reinhold Niebuhr

He who forgiveth, and is reconciled unto his enemy, shall receive his reward from God; for he loveth not the unjust doers.

the Koran

The ineffable joy of forgiving and being forgiven forms an ecstasy that might well arouse the envy of the gods.

Elbert Hubbard

Forgiveness is the most powerful thing you can do to get on the spiritual path. If you can't do it, you can forget about getting to higher levels of awareness and creating real magic in your life.

Wayne Dyer

Forgiveness does not change the past, but it does enlarge the future.

Paul Boese

When I feel betrayed by someone, instead of sulking, clinging to my resentment and playing the role of victim, I am challenged to strengthen my soul through forgiveness. By forgiving the person who hurt me, I strengthen my soul. . . . Each time we are called upon to forgive, we nourish our souls and learn more about who we are and what we have to share in this world. This is also an example of unconditional love.

John Gray

 Happiness

In his journals, Thomas Merton muses about happiness. "You can make of your life what you want. There are various ways of being happy. Why do we drive ourselves on with illusory demands? Happy only when we conform to something that is said to be a legitimate happiness? An approved happiness?" God gave us the freedom to create our own lives, he wrote, and, therefore, the freedom to create our own happiness. So why do we sometimes feel guilty about doing those things that make us happy? Especially if they vary from our family's or our society's definition of happiness? He wrote, "I am a happy person. God has given me happiness, but I am guilty about it—as if being happy were not quite allowed, as if everybody didn't have it within reach somehow or other."

Coretta Scott King shared, "I'm fulfilled in what I do. . . . I never thought that a lot of money or fine clothes—the finer things of life—would make you happy. My concept of happiness is to be filled in a spiritual sense." One way to connect with our spirituality is to define our own concept of happiness—to find out what makes us happy, and as long as it doesn't harm anyone, to pursue that happiness and allow it to fill us in the spiritual sense.

Happiness cannot be traveled to, owned, earned, worn, or consumed.
Happiness is the spiritual experience of living every minute with
love, grace, and gratitude.

Denis Waitley

Happiness radiates like the fragrance from a flower, and draws all
good things toward you. Allow your love to nourish yourself as well
as others. Do not strain after the needs of life. It is sufficient to be
quietly alert and aware of them. In this way life proceeds more
naturally and effortlessly. Life is here to Enjoy!

Maharishi Mahesh Yogi

Most of us experience happiness when we are enjoying life and feeling free, enjoying the process and products of our creative and intellectual processes, enjoying the ecstasy of transcendent oneness with the universe.

James Muriel

Happiness resides not in possessions and not in gold, the feeling of happiness dwells in the soul.

Democritus

Happiness is spiritual, born of Truth and Love. It is unselfish; therefore it cannot exist alone, but requires all mankind to share it.

Mary Baker Eddy

Look at the trees, look at the birds, look at the clouds, look at the stars . . . and if you have eyes you will be able to see that the whole existence is joyful. Everything is simply happy. Trees are happy for no reason; they are not going to become prime ministers or presidents and they are not going to become rich and they will never have any bank balance. Look at the flowers—for no reason. It is simply unbelievable how happy flowers are.

Osho

It is not God's will merely that we should be happy, but that we should make ourselves happy.

Immanuel Kant

The purpose of our lives is to be happy.

the Dalai Lama

Happiness is the realization of God in the heart.
Happiness is the result of praise and thanksgiving,
Of faith and acceptance;
A quiet, tranquil realization of the love of God.

White Eagle

There is a curriculum in living in which I have not studied. This may
be happiness. I want to know it; I should feel better prepared for
immortality. I do not wish to arrive fagged at last and a bit slipshod
in the spirit, as if I had a hard time all my mortal life. It is not
complimentary to God.

Corra Harris

Think of all the beauty that's still left in and around you and be happy!

Anne Frank

Home

The need for shelter is organic to all things natural, while the need for
home is organic to all things spiritual. Ralph Waldo Emerson wrote, "Every
spirit builds itself a house, and beyond its house a world, and beyond its
world a heaven." This is why our homes, if created with spirit, feel like our
own little worlds, our own slice of heaven. If we saw them not only as
functional places to live in, but spiritual places to flourish within, and if
we took care in designing them as if we were designing heaven itself, we
would find that our hours spent in them would be hours where our
bodies were sheltered while our spirits were at home.

Home is the definition of God.

Emily Dickinson

Home should be a place of nourishment, a place where we become physically, mentally, and spiritually refreshed: a sanctuary.

Nicole Marcelis

We shape our dwellings, and afterwards our dwellings shape us.

Winston Churchill

Establishing a home or business is always an act of natural religion, and if we don't bring appropriate sensitivity to the mystery, depth, and sacredness inherent in that activity, then we increase our disenchantment.

Thomas Moore

The dwellings we create and in which we abide (interiorly and exteriorly) manifest an aspect of our soul. The "places" of dreams and fantasies, the dwellings—high-rise apartments, old haunted mansions, basements, hallways, and bedrooms—tell us much about where our soul is at the moment.

Barbara Kirksey

Your house is your larger body. It grows in the sun and sleeps in the stillness of the night; and it is not dreamless. Does not your house dream?

Kahlil Gibran

When men do not love their hearth, nor reverence their thresholds, it is a sign that they have dishonoured both. . . . Our God is a house-hold God, as well as a heavenly one; He has an altar in every man's dwelling.

John Ruskin

A roof to keep out the rain. Four walls to keep out the wind. Floors to keep out the cold. Yes, but home is more than that. It is the laugh of a baby, the song of a mother, the strength of a father. Warmth of loving hearts, light from happy eyes, kindness, loyalty, comradeship. Home is first school and first church for the young ones, where they learn what is right, what is good, and what is kind. Where they go for comfort when they are hurt or sick. Where joy is shared and sorrow eased. Where fathers and mothers are respected and loved. Where children are wanted. Where the simplest food is good enough for kings because it is earned. Where money is not so important as loving-kindness. Where even the teakettle sings from happiness. That is home. God bless it.

Ernestine Schumann-Heink

Home is not just a place to sleep,
home is where we house our souls.

Alexandra Stoddard

To Adam, Paradise was home.
To the good among his descendants, home is paradise.

Julius Charles Hare

Home interprets heaven. Home is heaven for beginners.

Charles H. Parkhurst

If men lived like men indeed, their houses would be temples—temples which we should hardly dare to injure, and in which it would make us holy to be permitted to live.

John Ruskin

Hope

I love the term *hope chest*. Though I know the narrow historical meaning (they used to be called "marriage chests" and were for young women to place their linens and things inside until they married), I love the wider imaginal meaning, that inside of all our chests there lies hope tucked away. Some hopes are buried deep at the bottom of those chests, for they have been there forever, but other hopes are new, afterthoughts almost, placed on top for easy removal in case they should be replaced by new hopes. Some people keep their hope chests locked up because they feel too vulnerable to reveal the contents, but others will give you the key or open it for you and invite you to look inside. There, if you examine the contents of their hope chest with gentle eyes, you'll see revealed the magnitude of their spirit, because there is a sacred marriage between the human spirit and hope.

The word which God has written on the brow of every person is hope.

Victor Hugo

For God alone my soul waits in silence, for my hope is from Him.

Psalms 62:1

Hope, like faith, is nothing if it is not courageous;
it is nothing if it is not ridiculous.

Thornton Wilder

When we have hope, we are showing that we trust God to work out
the situation. Trust is the only way we're going to make it through
and be a part of God's marvelous plan for His child.

Barbara Johnson

"Hope" is the thing with feathers—
That perches in the soul—
And sings the tunes without the words—
And never stops—at all.

Emily Dickinson

Humans are, properly speaking, based upon hope, we have no other
possession but hope; this world of ours is emphatically the place of hope.

Thomas Carlyle

When the heart is enlivened again, it feels like the sun coming out after
a week of rainy days. There is hope in the heart that chases the clouds
away. Hope is a higher heart frequency and as you begin to reconnect
with your heart, hope is waiting to show you new possibilities and
arrest the downward spiral of grief and loneliness. It becomes a matter
of how soon you want the sun to shine. Listening to the still, small
voice in your heart will make hope into a reality.

Sara Paddison

Listen now to the gentle whispers of hope.

Charles D. Brodhead

The most important word in the English language is *hope*.

Eleanor Roosevelt

Strong hope is a much greater stimulant of life than
any single realized joy could be.

Friedrich Nietzsche

Hope is some extraordinary spiritual grace that God gives us
to control our fears, not to oust them.

Vincent McNabb

 Humility

Holy monk and man Thomas Merton believed "It is almost impossible to overestimate the value of true humility and its power in the spiritual life." In *New Seeds of Contemplation,* he wrote that "in perfect humility all selfishness disappears and your soul no longer lives for itself or in itself for God: and it is lost and submerged in Him and transformed into Him." He believed that "everyone who humbles himself is exalted" because the one who is humble "swims in the attributes of God, Whose power, magnificence, greatness, and eternity have, through love, through humility, become our own."

I love his description of a humble soul as one who "swims in the attributes of God." I might also liken that soul to one who basks in the sun of the spirit. Humble souls, if complimented on their suntan, don't take the glory for themselves but give it to the sun. They see themselves merely as reflectors for the magnificence of that sun, and they know that if they deserve any credit at all, it's only for their longing to "fly toward it," as Saint Thérèse of Lisieux wrote below. In becoming more spiritual, we do so with humility as our guide as we swim in the sea, or fly toward the sun, of the powerful and radiant Divine.

Lord Jesus, I am not an eagle.
All I have are the eyes and
The heart of one. In spite of my littleness,
I dare to gaze at the sun of love,
And I long to fly toward it.

Saint Thérèse of Lisieux

What is humility? It is that habitual quality whereby we live in the truth of things: the truth that we are creatures and not the Creator; the truth that our life is a composite of good and evil, light and darkness; the truth that in our littleness we have been given extravagant dignity. . . . Humility is saying a radical "yes" to the human condition.

Robert F. Morneau

What then is true humility? I would say humility is the opposite of pride which I dare say our perception of humility leads to. But if you want a blatant response I would describe humility as a *sincere* desire for the well-being of others, caring for others to the point that you would sacrifice your own gain for theirs, not so you look good to God but out of love. Where the idea came from that humility was being quiet, meek, and critical of yourself came from I don't know. In essence humility is an offshoot of love.

Derek Boldt

Whosoever therefore shall humble himself as this little child, the same is greatest in the kingdom of heaven.

Matthew 18:4

Pray
To be humble
So that God does not
Have to appear to be so stingy.

Hafiz

It was pride that changed angels into devils;
it is humility that makes men as angels.

Saint Augustine

Be humble and you will remain entire. The sages do not display themselves, therefore they shine. They do not approve themselves, therefore they are noted. They do not praise themselves, therefore they have merit. They do not glory in themselves, therefore they excel.

Lao Tzu

One must be as humble as the dust before he can discover truth.

Gandhi

True humility is intelligent self-respect which keeps us from thinking too highly or too meanly of ourselves. It makes us mindful of the nobility God meant us to have, yet it makes us modest by reminding us how far we have come short of what we can be.

Ralph W. Sockman

What makes humility so desirable is the marvelous thing it does to us; it creates in us a capacity for the closest possible intimacy with God.

Monica Baldwin

Would you be a pilgrim on the road to Love? The first condition is that you make yourself as humble as dust and ashes.

Ansari of Herat

 Kindness

Many people remember Aldous Huxley from reading his famous novel *Brave New World* in high school. Despite that novel's bleak vision of a futuristic dysutopian society, Huxley was a man who spent a lifetime studying and exploring the dimensions of the human spirit. On his deathbed, when he was asked for advice for humanity, he reportedly said, "All we need to do is to be a little kinder toward each other." I read that and think, "That's *all*?"

Beat generation writer Jack Kerouac said it in his own unique way: "By practicing kindness all over with everyone you will soon come into the holy trance, definite distinctions of personalities will become what they really mysteriously are, our common and eternal blissstuff, the pureness of everything forever, the great bright essence of mind, even and one thing everywhere the holy eternal milky love, the white light everywhere everything, emptybliss, svaya, shining, ready, and awake, the compassion in the sound of silence, the swarming myriad trillionaire you are." I read that and think, "All *that*?"

Then I think about kindness a little, and I know it's all, and it's all that.
The highest wisdom is kindness.

the Talmud

Kind words do not cost much. They never blister the tongue or lips.
They make other people good-natured. They also produce their own
image on men's souls, and a beautiful image it is.

Blaise Pascal

Let no one ever come to you without leaving better and happier.
Be the living expression of God's kindness: kindness in your face,
kindness in your eyes, kindness in your smile.

Mother Teresa

Life is short and we have never too much time for gladdening the
hearts of those who are traveling the dark journey with us.
Oh be swift to love, make haste to be kind.

Henri Frédéric Amiel

This is my simple religion. There is no need for temples; no need for complicated philosophy. Our own brain, our own heart is our temple; the philosophy is kindness.

the Dalai Lama

To give pleasure to a single heart by a single kind act is better than a thousand head-bowings in prayer.

Saddi

That best portion of a good man's life; his little, nameless, unremembered acts of kindness and love.

William Wordsworth

Neither genius, fame, nor love shows the greatness of the soul. Only kindness can do that.

Jean Baptiste Henri Lacordaire

Kind words are the music of the world. They have a power which seems to be beyond natural causes, as if they were some angel's song which had lost its way and come on earth. It seems as if they could almost do what in reality God alone can do—soften the hard and angry hearts of human beings. No one was ever corrected by a sarcasm—crushed, perhaps, if the sarcasm was clever enough, but drawn nearer to God, never.

Frederick William Faber

Kindness in words creates confidence.
Kindness in thinking creates profoundness.
Kindness in giving creates love.

Lao Tzu

Kindness is an essential part of God's work and ours here on earth.

Billy Graham

So many gods, so many creeds, so many paths . . . while just the act of being kind is all the world needs.

Ella Wheeler Wilcox

Three things in human life are important: the first is to be kind. The second is to be kind. The third is to be kind.

Henry James

 Listening

In the section on Seeing, the distinction was made between seeing and *seeing*, though we use the same word for both. In the case of the difference between hearing and listening, though we have two separate words, the distinction is the same. One of my favorite Sufi poets, Jalaluddin Rumi, refers constantly to the importance of listening, and in particular, of listening with the ear in the center of the chest, from where the Divine speaks. "Give more of your life to this listening," he tells us, so we can hear from "the one who talks to the deep ear in your chest." He advises us to "sell [our] tongues and buy a thousand ears when that one steps near and begins to speak." My other beloved Sufi poet, Hafiz, advises us on how to listen to others.

How
Do I
Listen to others?
As if everyone were my Master

Speaking to me
His
Cherished
Last
Words.

Learn to listen like that, and you can't help but hear the Divine speak.

God speaks in the silence of the heart.
Listening is the beginning of prayer.

Mother Teresa

To deepen my experience of God, I take time to listen. I listen to the wind, I listen to the birds, I listen to the sacred. I open up to feeling humble. I open up to feeling the magic of life. I'm just in awe of the radiance of life that surrounds us every day.

Lynne Andrews

All things and all men, so to speak, call on us with small or loud voices. They want us to listen, they want us to understand their intrinsic claims, their justice of being. . . . But we can give it to them only through the love that listens. . . . The first duty of love is to listen.

Paul Tillich

Listening is the oldest and perhaps the most powerful tool of healing. It is often through the quality of our listening and not the wisdom of our words that we are able to effect the most profound changes in the people around us.

Rachel Naomi Remen

Listening is a rare happening among human beings. You cannot listen to the word another is speaking if you are preoccupied with your appearance, or with impressing the other, or are trying to decide what you are going to say when the other stops talking, or are debating about whether what is being said is true or relevant or agreeable. Such matters have their place, but only after listening to the word as the word is being uttered. Listening is a primitive act of love in which a person gives himself to another's word, making himself accessible and vulnerable to that word.

William Stringfellow

To love is to listen; to listen is to love.

Mary Watkins

Hearing is one of the body's five senses, but listening is an art.

Frank Tyger

 Love

How does one write an introduction to love? I know there's nothing I can say about it that will amplify love's importance as a spiritual path and practice, and I'm more afraid whatever I say will somehow diminish it. One of the most exquisite and elegant passages I've ever read about love was written by psychologist Carl Jung. "In my medical experience as well as in my own life I have again and again been faced with the mystery of love and have never been able to explain what it is. . . . Men can try to name love, showering upon it all the names at his command, and still he will involve himself in endless self-deceptions. If he possesses a grain of wisdom, he will lay down his arms and name the unknown by the more unknown, *ignotum per ignotious*—that is, by the name of God."

With a grain of wisdom and a silo of humility, I lay down my arms and offer the words of others on the power of love, on the importance of loving others, and on loving and being loved by the Divine.

THE POWER OF LOVE

Never forget that the most powerful force on earth is love.

Nelson Rockefeller

It is for love that the whole universe sprang into existence,
and it is for the sake of love that it is kept going.

Meher Baba

I gave my soul to him
And all the things I owned were his:
I have no flock to tend
Nor any other trade
And my one ministry is love.

Saint John of the Cross

Perhaps the old monks were right when they tried to root love out;
perhaps the poets are right when they try to water it. It is a blood-red
flower, with the color of sin; but there is always the scent of
a god about it.

Olive Schreiner

Insomuch as love grows in you so in you beauty grows.
For love is the beauty of the soul.

Saint Augustine

You can search throughout the entire universe for someone who is more deserving of your love and affection than you are yourself, and that person is not to be found anywhere. You yourself, as much as anybody in the entire universe, deserve your love and affection.

Buddha

To love very much is to love inadequately; we love—that is all. Love cannot be modified without being nullified. Love is a short word but it contains everything. Love means the body, the soul, the life, the entire being. We feel love as we feel the warmth of our blood, we breathe love as we breathe the air, we hold it in ourselves as we hold our thoughts. Nothing more exists for us. Love is not a word; it is a wordless state indicated by four letters.

Guy de Maupassant

All thoughts, all passions, all delights,
Whatever stirs this mortal frame,
Are all ministers of Love,
And feed his sacred flame.

Samuel Taylor Coleridge

Love is not a cool arrangement or a night in bed. Love is angels hovering, circling, calling us to seek the sky together.

Marianne Williamson

Love is life. All, everything that I understand I understand only because I love. Everything is, everything exists, only because I love. Everything is united by it alone. Love is God, and to die means that I, a particle of love, shall return to the general and eternal source.

Leo Tolstoy

Through love we are destroyed and re-created. This is the ancient mystery of the Sufi path. To reach God you have to be turned inside out burnt with the fire of love until nothing remains but the ashes.

Llewellyn Vaughan-Lee

Love is the god of gods, and no god is greater than love.

Johannes Secundus

Your religion is where your love is.

Albert Einstein

Love is the light that dissolves all walls between souls, families, and nations.

Paramahansa Yogananda

In every moment of genuine love, we are dwelling in God and God is dwelling in us.

Paul Tillich

Love is the most universal, the most tremendous, and the most mysterious of the cosmic forces.

Pierre Teilhard de Chardin

LOVING OTHERS

. . . if we love one another, God lives in us and His love is made complete in us.

1 John 4:12

Love all God's creation, the whole and every grain of sand in it. Love every leaf, every ray of God's light. Love the animals, love the plants, love everything. If you love everything, you will perceive the divine mystery in things. Once you perceive it, you will begin to comprehend it better every day. And you will come at last to love the whole world with an all-embracing love.

Fyodor Dostoyevsky

Who loves all beings, without distinction,
He indeed is worshipping best his God.

Swami Vivekananda

A religious awakening which does not awaken the sleeper
to love has roused him in vain.

Jessamyn West

We cannot see God himself, but we can see him as he has chosen to reveal himself in [those] who inspire love in our hearts.

Ib'n al-Arabi

The best way to know God is to love many things.

Vincent van Gogh

Make many acts of love, for they set the soul on fire and make it gentle.

Saint Teresa of Avila

Loving with abandon is our spiritual tendency.

Jim Rosemergy

If you have a particular faith or religion, that is good.
But you can survive without it if you have a love, compassion,
and tolerance. The clear proof of a person's love of God is
if that person genuinely shows love to fellow human beings.

the Dalai Lama

LOVING AND BEING LOVED BY THE DIVINE

The soul is made of love and must ever strive to return to love.
Therefore, it can never find rest nor happiness in other things. It must
lose itself in love. By its very nature it must seek God, who is love.

Mechthild of Magdeburg

There are many who want me to tell them of secret ways of becoming
perfect and I can only tell them that the sole secret is a hearty love of
God, and the only way of attaining that love is by loving. You learn to
speak by speaking, to study by studying, to run by running, to work
by working; and just so you learn to love God and man by loving.
Begin as a mere apprentice and the very power of love will lead
you on to become a master of the art.

Saint Francis de Sales

I, God, am in your midst.
Whoever knows me can never fall,
Not in the heights,
Nor in the depths,
Nor in the breadths,
For I am love,
Which the vast expanses of evil
Can never still.

Hildegard of Bingen

Love seeks no cause beyond itself and no fruit; it is its own fruit, its own enjoyment. I love because I love; I love in order that I love. Of all the motions and affections of the soul, love is the only one by means of which the creature, (though not in equal terms) is able to create with the creator and to give back something resembling what has been given to it. When God loves, He only desires to be loved, knowing that love will render all those who love Him happy.

Saint Bernard of Clairveaux

The spiritual journey isn't quick, or easy, but I am propelled by knowing the God within me, the Divine Love that is our essential nature. And so I walk the path that I've chosen at some deep and unknowable level. As I am able and willing to heal my own through living in Divine Love, I become an able instrument for a greater good wanting to emerge on this Earth and in all people.

Meredith L. Young-Sowers

Everything I learned in my first forty-two years was but preparation for my love affair with Spirit. Love is the goal, love is the path, love is the lesson, love is the joy, love is the pain, love is the teacher.

Kenny Loggins

The love of God, unutterable and perfect,
flows into a pure soul the way that light
rushes into a transparent object.
The more love that it finds, the more it gives itself;
so that, as we grow clear and open,
the more complete the joy of heaven is.
And the more souls who resonate together,
the greater the intensity of their love,
and, mirror-like, each soul reflects the other.

Dante Alighieri

When we acquaint ourselves with the Divine,
We discover that the nature of God is Love,
and we see that Love is the creative Principle of Life.

H. B. Jeffrey

Questioning

There is a detail in one of the versions of the Arthurian legend concerning the search for the Holy Grail that has always fascinated me. The Holy Grail was thought to be the cup that Jesus drank from at the Last Supper, the same cup that Joseph of Arimithea used later to gather the blood from the body of the crucified Christ. The Grail had miraculous powers, including the power to heal. Percival, a young and eager man hoping to reach knighthood, went off in search of the Grail. It was in the possession of the Fisher King, who was terribly wounded, and as a result, the country he ruled had fallen into a wasteland. Percival stumbled upon the king's castle and that night was shown the Grail, but he said nothing. The next morning he awakened to an empty castle. Mystified, he rode away into the forest, where he met a maiden who told him that all he had to do to heal the king and the country was to ask questions concerning the Grail, particularly the question of "whom one served with it." He vowed to seek the Grail again, and the next time, to ask the right questions.

This myth illustrates the value of asking questions on our way to fulfilling our quest for the Holy Grail. It shows that a questioning spirit will lead us to that which is Holy and which has the potential to heal, to make whole again.

Being religious means asking passionately the question of the
meaning of our existence and being willing to receive answers,
even if the answers hurt.

Paul Tillich

It is not the answer that enlightens, but the question.

Decouvertes

The important thing is not to stop questioning. Curiosity has its own reason for existing. One cannot help but be in awe when he contemplates the mysteries of eternity, of life, of the marvelous structure of reality. It is enough if one tries merely to comprehend a little of this mystery every day. Never lose a holy curiosity.

Albert Einstein

Our lives are made up of a series of mysteries that we are meant to explore but that are meant to remain unsolved. We are meant to live with the questions we have about our lives, even use them as companions, and allow them to lead us into the deepest recesses of our nature, wherein we discover the sacred.

Caroline Myss

The meaning of my existence is that life has addressed a question to me. Or, conversely, I myself am a question which is addressed to the world, and I must communicate my answer. . . . I also think of the possibility that through the achievement of an individual a question enters the world, to which he must provide some kind of answer.

Carl Jung

I am prejudiced in favor of him who, without impudence, can ask boldly. He has faith in humanity, and faith in himself. No one who is not accustomed to giving grandly can ask nobly and with boldness.

Johann Kaspar Lavater

Questions are the creative acts of intelligence.

Frank Kingdom

How is one to live a moral and compassionate existence when one is fully aware of the blood, the horror inherent in life, when one finds darkness not only in one's culture but within oneself? If there is a stage at which an individual life becomes truly adult, it must be when one grasps the irony in its unfolding and accepts responsibility for a life lived in the midst of such paradox. One must live in the middle of contradiction, because if all contradiction were eliminated at once life would collapse. There are simply no answers to some of the great pressing questions. You continue to live them out, making your life a worthy expression of leaning into the light.

Barry Lopez

 Service

One of my favorite quotes on service is by Russian writer Leo Tolstoy, who wrote, "The sole meaning of life is to serve humanity." However, years ago, when I copied it into my quote book, somehow I wrote it as "The *soul* meaning of life is to serve humanity." Years later, unsure of my own transcription, I did some research to find out the original wording.

Tolstoy did use the word *sole,* but I think he would be pleased with the pun and would agree that serving others is our soul's meaning. I have consistently found that there is no road more royal, nor path so straight and true to connecting with my own soul's meaning and purpose as that of serving the soul of the world, in all ways great and small.

The best way to find yourself is to lose yourself in the service of others.

Gandhi

No man has ever risen to the real stature of spiritual manhood
until he has found that it is kinder to serve somebody else than
it is to serve himself.

Woodrow Wilson

It is a privilege to serve mankind, for this is the worship of God;
God is here, in all these human souls. He is the soul of man.

Swami Vivekananda

They are the real lovers of God
Who feel others' sorrow as their own.
When they perform selfless service,
They are humble servants of the Lord.
Respecting all, despising none,
They are pure in thought, word, and deed.

Narsinha Mehta

Each day do some good. Give to a worthy cause, it doesn't matter
how much; or help some individual. God is watching to see if you
feel for his suffering in others. Make up your mind to be of service
to someone every day. You can often help others just by giving them
a little understanding. Never gloat over the faults of wayward
brothers if you wish to reform them. See God in everyone, as
I see him. Do not ridicule an erring person. God is sleeping
in that soul; you must lovingly awaken him.

Paramahansa Yogananda

There is no higher religion than human service.
To work for the common good is the greatest creed.

Albert Schweitzer

When you ignore your soul's destiny, when you get caught up in your own self-interests and forget to care for others, you will not feel "right." Instead, you will feel empty and unfulfilled. During these times, you are neglecting your soul—you are depriving it of nourishment. . . . seek something outside your nine-to-five job as an additional source of fulfillment and as a way to feel the joy of helping others. You can do any number of things to fulfill this goal—volunteer at a community hotline, coach a Little League team, donate your time to a public school, visit the sick. Whatever you choose, you will gain a sense that you are giving of yourself, that you are sharing yourself with the world, that you are fulfilling the destiny of your soul.

Rabbi Harold Kushner

I slept and dreamt that life was joy
I awoke and saw that life was service
I acted and behold, service was joy.

Rabindranath Tagore

These people care. And care is love and love is service
and service is Salvation.

Louise Imogen Guiney

Whoever would be great among you must be your servant.

Matthew 20:26

Everybody can be great . . . because anybody can serve. You don't have to have a college degree to serve. You don't have to make your subject and verb agree to serve. You only need a heart full of grace. A soul generated by love.

Martin Luther King, Jr.

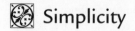 Simplicity

The great architect Frank Lloyd Wright said, "It is a *spiritual* thing to comprehend what simplicity means." This seems to be true. When you think about some of the people you most associate with spirituality—Jesus, Buddha, Gandhi, Mother Teresa, Lao Tzu, the saints and monks and nuns—they all led and lead lives of voluntary simplicity. In fact, there are many stories of wealthy and worldly people who renounced their riches for a life of simplicity—the prime example being Prince Siddhartha, who walked away from a palace of unbelievable wealth and the path of kingly power to pursue enlightenment through renunciation of worldly possessions and became the Buddha. However, there are few stories of someone going the opposite direction, from rags to riches, and gaining genuine spirituality. Socrates understood this when he taught, "The fewer our wants, the more we resemble the gods."

What Richard Gregg wrote of voluntary simplicity leads us to understand its gifts. "Voluntary simplicity involves both inner and outer conditions. It means singleness of purpose, sincerity and honesty within, as well as avoidance of exterior clutter, of many possessions irrelevant to the chief purpose of life. It means an ordering and guiding of our energy and our desires, a partial restraint in some directions in order to secure greater abundance of life in other directions. It involves a deliberate organization of life for a purpose." If our purpose in life is to increase and enhance our connection to spiritual energy, it seems clear that simplicity paves the way.

The ability to simplify means to eliminate the unnecessary
so that the necessary may speak.

Hans Hofmann

God always takes the simplest way.

Albert Einstein

The pastoral vision of simplicity has much appeal to those of us in the West for whom life can be full of confusion, distraction, and complexity. In the rush of modern industrial society and in the attempt to maintain our image as successful persons, we feel that we have lost touch with a deeper, more profound part of our being. Yet we feel that we have little time, energy, or cultural support to pursue these areas of life that we know are important. We long for a simpler way of life that allows us to restore some balance to our lives.

Duane Elgin

Our life is frittered away by detail. Simplify, simplify, simplify! I say, let your affairs be as two or three, and not a hundred or a thousand; instead of a million count half a dozen, and keep your accounts on your thumb-nail.

Henry David Thoreau

Manifest plainness, Embrace simplicity, Reduce selfishness, Have few desires.

Lao Tzu

I am beginning to learn that it is the sweet, simple things of life which are the real ones after all.

Laura Ingalls Wilder

Beauty of style and harmony and grace and good rhythm depend on simplicity.

Plato

O holy simplicity!

John Russ

Live simply that others may simply live.

Gandhi

Aspire to simple living? That means, aspire to fulfill the highest human destiny.

Charles Wagner

I have the greatest of all riches: that of not desiring them.

Eleanora Duse

If my hands are fully occupied in holding on to something, I can neither give nor receive.

Dorothee Solle

The art of art, the glory of expression and the sunshine of the light of letters is simplicity; nothing is better than simplicity.

Walt Whitman

 Solitude

Yesterday my mother kissed me good-bye and wished me luck and productivity during my time of "solitary confinement." I was leaving for a little cottage on the coast that my longtime friend Michael owns and so graciously offers to friends needing to get away.

Less than a day into my sojourn, I find myself awed again by how easy it is through intentional solitude to experience the deeper depths of my soul, and the higher heights of my spirit, experiences that are sometimes flattened out in the city with all its cacophony, and in companionship with all its commitments and considerations. Here the only sounds are those of nature; here my sole companion is my soul; here I come to understand how "solitary confinement" can actually release the imprisoned spirit; and here I am reminded once again of the importance of occasional spiritual sojourns to solitary places as well as making place and space for solitude in our everyday lives.

I am often asked if I am not lonely on my solitary excursions.
It seems so self-evident that one cannot be lonesome where
everything is wild and beautiful and busy and steeped with
God that the question is hard to answer.

John Muir

Solitude is the furnace of transformation.

Henri Nouwen

A certain amount of quiet alone time, whether it is spent meditating,
exercising, reading, listening to music, or being creative is, I think,
essential for the mental health of most human beings.

Barbara Powell

There is nothing either/or about being alone, because it is not a role.
It is not a reduced way of life. It is a possibility for us to participate
in a highly creative endeavor: the discovery of our whole selves.

Phyllis Hobe

It is sometimes said that each of us is ultimately alone. That idea is
compelling not because of birth and death but because so often our
moments alone seem more true, more real. The word "God" only
begins to have meaning for me when I am alone. Or if not alone, so
at one with another that there is no sense of a competing reality. God
has no meaning for me in a discussion. I don't think religion is an
attainable subject for the intellect. I can only believe when I'm not
talking about it. I need solitude like I need food and rest, and like
eating and resting, solitude is most healing when it fits the rhythm of
my needs. A rigidly scheduled aloneness does not nourish me. Solitude
is perhaps a misnomer. To me, being alone means togetherness—the
re-coming-together of myself and nature, of myself and being; the
reuniting of my self with all other selves. Solitude especially means
putting the parts of my mind back together, unifying the pieces
of my self scattered by anger and fear, until I can once again
see that the little things are little and the big things are big.

Hugh Prather

Genuine tranquility of the heart and perfect peace of mind, the
highest blessings on earth after health, are to be found only in solitude
and, as a permanent disposition, only in the deepest seclusion.

Arthur Schopenhauer

Only when one is connected to one's inner core is one connected
to others. And, for me, the core, the inner spring, can best be
re-found through solitude.

Anne Morrow Lindbergh

Whosoever is delighted in solitude is either a wild beast or a god.

Francis Bacon

You need not leave your room. Remain sitting at your table and listen. You need not even listen, simply wait, just learn to become quiet, and still, and solitary. The world will freely offer itself to you to be unmasked. It has no choice; it will roll in ecstasy at your feet.

Franz Kafka

I should be able to return to solitude each time as to the place I have never described to anybody, as to the place which I never brought anyone to see, as the place whose silence has mothered an interior life known to no one but God alone.

Thomas Merton

 Truth

According to Hinduism, there are four general kinds of people with four different dispositions, and for each different personality type, a different path, known as a *yoga,* exists to follow for the realization of the Divine. *Jnana yoga* is for persons with a strong intellectual disposition; it is the path to the Divine through knowledge or wisdom. It is a particular kind of knowledge—the knowledge of the ultimate truth—and is broken into three parts: hearing the truth, reflecting on that truth, and realizing the truth through unbroken meditation, which ultimately brings *samadhi,* or union with the Divine.

I love what South African writer Nadine Gordimer says about truth: "The truth isn't always beauty, but the hunger for it is." It echoes one of my favorite Tracy Chapman songs, where she sings "hunger only for a taste of justice; hunger only for a world of truth." People who practice *jnana yoga* have a hunger for the truth. And anyone can practice *jnana yoga,* Hindu or not, for as many of the quotes below illustrate, truth is not to be found in one doctrine or one religion but is more likely to be found within the heart and soul of the one who seeks it with all of his or her heart and soul.

The piece of advice that I find extremely helpful is one attributed to a group called the "Sarmouni Brotherhood." It says, "There is no God but Reality. To seek Him elsewhere is the action of the Fall." To me, this means you need to seek for *truth* first. Whenever you put your ideas about how things are ahead of actually trying to see what's really there you're inevitably going to create trouble. No matter how you'd like things to be ideally, you have to keep coming back and checking in with what actually *is.*

Charles Tart

Whoever multiplies words causes confusion.
The truth that can be spoken
is not the Ultimate Truth.
Ultimate Truth is wordless,
the silence within the silence.

Pirke Avot

Whatever satisfies the soul is truth.

Walt Whitman

And I will ask the Father, and he will give you another counselor to be with you forever—the spirit of truth. The world cannot accept him, because it neither sees him nor knows him. But you will know him, for he lives with you and will be in you.

John 14:16–17

Truth is not a word, it is not a concept; it isn't your truth and my truth, the Christian truth and the Muslim truth. Truth, like love, has no nationality, but to love and to see truth there must be no hate, no jealousy, no division, and no anger.

Jiddu Krishnamurti

In proportion as we perceive and embrace the truth we do become just, heroic, magnanimous, divine.

William Lloyd Garrison

Keep one thing forever in view—the truth; and if you do this, though it may seem to lead you away from the opinion of people, it will assuredly conduct you to the throne of God.

Horace Mann

It is the great work of nature to transmute sunlight into life. So it is the great end of Christian living to transmute the light of truth into the fruits of holy living.

Adoniram J. Gordon

Truth is the beginning of every good thing, both in heaven and on earth; and the person who would be blessed and happy should be from the first a partaker of truth, for then that person can be trusted.

Plato

It is noble to seek truth, and it is beautiful to find it. It is the ancient feeling of the human heart—that knowledge is better than riches; and it is deeply and sacredly true.

Sydney Smith

Understanding

When I was a child, one of my favorite books was called *Tell Me Why*. No doubt it was written on the behest of some exasperated parents who were badgered by their offspring's asking them questions like "Why is the sky blue?" and "Why do mosquito bites itch?"

When small children all possess a quality, we can trust that there is something innately human about it, rather than something taught by their specific culture. Thus, the quest for understanding is natural. As any parent of a young child can tell you, however, there are times you wish they would stop already with the questions, not because you don't find them valuable or interesting or charming, but simply because you are frustrated by not knowing the answer. Thus, being frustrated by not understanding is also natural!

The Bible teaches us that there's a peace that passes all understanding, and that's true, that sometimes peace lies in understanding that it's okay that we don't understand. However, it's also true that there's an understanding that leads us to peace. For inside of us lives both a child who seeks peace through understanding, and an adult who finds peace without understanding, and both relationships to understanding can bring us nearer to our spirituality.

> Mystery creates wonder, and wonder is the
> basis of man's desire to understand.
>
> Neil Armstrong

> He who knows nothing, loves nothing. He who can do nothing
> understands nothing. He who understands nothing is worthless.
> But he who understands also loves, notices, sees. . . . The more
> knowledge is inherent in a thing, the greater the love.
>
> Paracelsus

Love comes into being when we understand the total
process of ourselves, and the understanding of ourselves
is the beginning of wisdom.

Jiddu Krishnamurti

In each of us is a seed of understanding. The seed is God.

Thich Nhat Hanh

And even as each one of you stands alone in God's knowledge,
so must each one of you be alone in his knowledge of God
and in his understanding of the earth.

Kahlil Gibran

Men are admitted into heaven not because they have curbed and
governed their passions or have no passions, but because they have
cultivated their understandings. The treasures of heaven are not
negations of passion, but relishes of intellect, from which all the
passions emanate uncurbed in their eternal glory.

William Blake

There is one purpose to life and one only: to bear witness to and
understand as much as possible of the complexity of the world—its
beauty, its mysteries, its riddles. The more you understand, the more
you look, the greater is your enjoyment of life and your sense of peace.
That's all there is to it. If an activity is not grounded in "to love"
or "to learn," it does not have value.

Anne Rice

The ultimate function of civilization is to serve the unfolding
of ever deeper spiritual understanding.

Arnold Toynbee

When you are deluded and full of doubt, even a thousand books
of scripture are not enough. When you have realized understanding,
even one word is too much.

Fen-Yang

 # Wonder

Recently I took a break from some particularly mundane work and went
to get my car washed. After sitting down in the long hallway full of windows
facing the mechanical part of the car wash, I opened a book on spirituality
that I brought, hoping to find some inspiration to make it through the
remainder of my day.

Down at the end of the hallway, a father lifted his two children up to
the windows to show them their truck coming through the wash. At each
new stage, he yelled loudly "WOW!" and they would repeat "WOW!"
"WOW!" Then he would put them down, run with them to the next set
of windows, lift them up, yell again "WOW! WOW!" until they replied in
even louder voices, "WOW! WOW! WOW!"

All of this was not wowing me. *It's a car wash, for God's sake, not one of the
Seven Wonders of the World,* I thought. I found myself annoyed, unable to
concentrate on my book, wanting to admonish them to "use your inside
voices."

It is amazing how shockingly unspiritual we spiritual seekers can sometimes be.

I had my inspiration, and the only person I had to admonish was myself.
Wow.

What is the future? What is the past? What are we? What is the magic
fluid that surrounds us and conceals the things we most need to
know? We live and die in the midst of marvels.

Napoleon Bonaparte

The universe shivers with wonder in the depths of the human.

Brian Swimme

He who can no longer pause to wonder and stand rapt in awe
is as good as dead; his eyes are closed.

Albert Einstein

I experience God in all situations that evoke awe in me. This frequently
occurs in nature, particularly in the mountains or the desert. It also
occurs in the arts, particularly music, poetry, theater, and painting.
These art forms frequently inspire me to feel great awe. In such
moments, I feel a communion with the Ultimate.

David Steindl-Rast

The most fortunate are those who have a wonderful capacity to
appreciate again and again, freshly and naively, the basic goods of life,
with awe, pleasure, wonder, and even ecstasy.

Abraham Maslow

I still find each day too short for all the thoughts I want to think,
all the walks I want to take, all the books I want to read, and all the
friends I want to see. The longer I live the more my mind dwells upon
the beauty and wonder of the world. I hardly know which feeling leads,
wonderment or admiration.

John Burroughs

It amazes me, and I know the wind will surely someday blow it all away
It amazes me, and I'm so very grateful that You made the world this way.

John Denver

The highest point a person can attain is not Knowledge, or Virtue, or
Goodness, or Victory, but something even greater, more heroic, and
more despairing: Sacred Awe!

Nikos Kazantzakis

For wonder leaps upon me still,
And makes me dizzy, makes me ill,
But never frightened—for I know—
Not where—but in whose hands I go:
The lovely fingers of delight
Have hold of me and hold me tight.

Edna St. Vincent Millay

We die on the day when our lives cease to be illumined by
the steady radiance, renewed daily, of a wonder, the source
of which is beyond all reason.

Dag Hammarskjöld

Wonder is the basis of worship.

Thomas Carlyle

Stuff your eyes with wonder, live as if you'd drop dead in
ten seconds. See the world. It's more fantastic than any
dream made or paid for in factories.

Ray Bradbury